Serge
ART

Krause Publications

700 East State St., Iola, WI 54990-0001
Telephone (715) 445-2214
www.krause.com

Please call or write for our free catalog of publications. Our toll-free number to place an order or obtain a free catalog is 800-258-0929 or please use our regular business telephone 715-445-2214 for editorial comment and further information.

Printed in the United States of America

Library of Congress Catalog Number: 98-86783

ISBN 0-87341-705-4

Dedication

*In memory of Dale Stoddard,
Mary Scarborough, and Dena Burns. I wish
you all could be here to see it come true.*

Acknowledgments

I have so many people to thank who have helped me get to this point and have been there through the years. Naming them all would be a whole book in itself so I have narrowed it down to the following.

Personally I would like to thank:

My mom, Betty Guidry. You started all this. There aren't enough words to thank you for everything.

My family - James, my daughter Jennifer and her Parrish, my son John and his Holly - for understanding and tolerating my extensive sewing and textile collection. My three grandkids who have given me so much joy and unconditional love, Sweety Petey (aka Rachel), Angel Baby (aka Ashlyn), and "THE BOY" (aka Evan).

My best friend, Nancy Broadway, for help with everything through thick and thin.

Mary Scarborough for being a once in a lifetime friend.

Dena Burns for having faith in me and nudging me along.

My two favorite professors at the University of Houston, John Hall and John Hummel, who required so many term papers. They prepared me well for this undertaking.

Professionally I would like to thank:

Carol McKinney for letting me use her beautiful garments for the chapter on Peek-a-Boo Pleats. She just oozes creativity.

Judy Pryor, my business partner, for taking care of so much while I was underground trying to meet the deadline.

Belle Harding for proofreading and invaluable suggestions for this book.

The "Material Girls," Jo Largent, Mary Nell Johnson, Fran Phillips, Sabrina Szymczyk, and Nancy Bray, for being such talented guinea pigs.

Connie Hoke who has become a whiz at her serger and loaned me her wonderful garments for photos in this book.

Everyone who has ever taken one of my classes. They have been the reason for all this.

Extreme thanks to everyone who has ever let me teach in their store.

Emily Austin and Mary Nell Johnson for the cameras.

My editor, Barbara Case, who never got on mine. She patiently answered a steady stream of questions.

Judy Bishop for being a friend and having such great designs for me to embellish with my serger, and also for good advice.

Judy Murrah and all her Jazz. Her books have greatly inspired me and given me a starting point for many serger embellishments.

Robbie Fanning, for taking time out of her busy schedule to share her knowledge and advice.

Of course, I couldn't have made it without the wonderful music of Steve Perry, Bruce Hornsby, Peter Kater, and R. Carlos Nakai. I may have to replace my CDs. They have played constantly.

Many thanks to the following companies who provided materials and sergers to use for samples and photos:

American & Efird, Inc.
DARR, Inc.
Dream World Enterprises Inc.
Elna USA
Husqvarna/Viking
Janome/New Home
Juki Union Special
Omnigrid
Pfaff American Sales Corp.
Robison-Anton Textile Company
SEW-ERGO
Sulky of America
Tacony - Babylock
ThreadPRO
YLI Corporation

Preface

One day about 12 years ago my mom gave me her sewing machine and everything she owned related to sewing. She said she was tired of sewing and didn't want to keep any of it. I made her keep a pair of scissors, just in case. A few weeks later, she called and asked me if I wanted to run around for the day and maybe go look at these funny looking machines called sergers. I bet you can guess what my answer was. Well, my mom surprised me that day with an early birthday present and I came home with a brand new serger. The salesman

took it out of the box and put white thread on it for me before we left. For a few weeks, I used that white thread on everything I made. (I still have a beautiful maroon blouse hanging in the spare closet made with that white thread.) I lived in constant fear that the thread would break. Since I was in graduate school studying to be a marriage and family therapist, I figured I should deal with that fear and get over it.

I started staying up all night playing with my serger instead of studying. I pinned samples of every stitch, along with the settings, in a notebook. Pretty soon I was really comfortable with that little machine. Within a few months I was teaching serger classes for a local sewing machine dealer. And the rest, as they say, is history.

By the way, that serger is still in use. Both of my kids have tried to talk me out of it but I have a hard time parting with it. And I still haven't finished graduate school. Probably never will.

Table of Contents

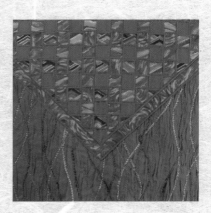

Introduction

Wearable art is everywhere, from the runways in Paris to the racks at the local discount department store. I really enjoy serging and making wearable art. Combining the two lets me have the best of both worlds. It enables me to create one-of-a-kind garments with lots of color and glitz in an amazingly short amount of time.

The introduction of the home serger has given sewing a tremendous boost in popularity in the past 15 years. Many people say they wouldn't be sewing today if everything still looked homemade with raw or zigzag stitch seam allowances. I feel the same way about that homemade look. I love the professionally finished look produced by using a serger. That is how my passion for serging began. Fascination with this nifty little machine and what it can do has become my career.

Teaching serger classes has given me the opportunity to stretch the limits of what a serger will do. Several years ago I started using the term "SergeArt" to distinguish my wearable art classes from my serger club and serger project classes. The garments in this book were designed to be projects in my SergeArt classes.

The garments I design use certain features of the serger that everyone can master with practice. The dozen garments featured in this book are designed for sergers of all skill levels. The instructions only deal with serger embellishments, not final garment construction. The technique instructions are generic so you will need to have your serger manual handy. Methods for final vest construction on the serger are covered in Chapter 4.

I have not included a comprehensive listing of every type of serger stitch but have provided definitions and general instructions for the serger techniques used to make the 12 garments featured. There are many great serger books available that cover the basics (see the Bibliography). This book is intended to blend and be used along with information found in other serger books. By combining the techniques in this book with those found in the others, you will have an endless combination of embellishments to use on your own creations.

The projects in this book are merely a starting point. You can't get all the information you need to know about serging from only one book. Many of my inspirations and ideas are obtained by looking through books. Judy Murrah's *Jacket Jazz* books have been a source for many of my ideas. I have taught many classes on her techniques for the sewing machine and I really enjoy the challenge of adapting sewing machine embellishments for the serger.

I hope you have as much fun creating and wearing your SergeArt garments as I do.

Sergingly Sew,
    Diane Bossom

Visit my serger website, Diane Bossom's Serger Place at
http://www.sergerplace.com

CHAPTER 1

Going on a Creative Journey

SergeArt - Wearable Art
On the Serger

It's the journey, not the destination. This saying has become so popular it is even being used in TV commercials. Well that comment is far from the truth when it comes to creative serging. You can enjoy *both* the journey of creating and the destination of wearing your own beautiful SergeArt garments. This chapter addresses many steps necessary before actually cutting any fabric. These basic steps will help you make a wonderfully wearable SergeArt creation.

For the best results, please read all instructions before starting any of the projects. You can follow the instructions and duplicate the garment or use the techniques that you like and create a garment of your own design. Incorporate the quick and easy techniques you can do on a serger into creating an entire SergeArt wardrobe.

Pick your favorite pattern or a pattern similar to the project garment and embellish it with SergeArt. Instructions are included for all the serger techniques used for the projects in this book. Most projects involve using both a serger and sewing machine. The majority of the decorative techniques are done on the serger. Instructions are also included for the sewing machine techniques.

One of the most important things about creative serging is to do what you enjoy. I always stress that personal preference is the best guide for enjoying what you create. If there are techniques you just don't like, then just don't do them.

Creative serging is a wonderful way to discover what your personal preferences are. There is such a huge array of fabric, threads, and yarns available to today's sewers that it is sometimes hard to narrow down the choices. Let your personal preference be your guide on your creative journey.

Serger Smarts

Not all sergers are created equal. There are different features on models within the same brand. Considering how many brands there are, you will get an idea of how difficult it is to give information that applies to all sergers. The manual is the only source for specific instructions for your serger. Become familiar with how to find specific information in your manual. Chapter 3 addresses serger basics in more depth.

People in classes often express some dissatisfaction with

their serging skills. They evaluate their serging abilities based on their sewing machine skills. This is not a fair comparison because most serger owners are much more experienced at using a sewing machine. A serger is very different from a sewing machine. The two kinds of machines operate differently. The body mechanics for operating a serger are different from those used for a sewing machine. The trick is to learn to operate a serger on its own terms and not treat it like a sewing machine. This is not an instant process. You have to learn how to handle a serger to get the most out of it.

What do you do with all that thread? Think of it like having to thread your sewing machine several times in a row. Each threading path is color coded. Most sergers have a picture inside the front cover to help with threading. There will definitely be diagrams in the manual. Deal with only one thread at a time and you won't feel overwhelmed. Look in the manual for the recommended threading order and always follow it.

Most important of all, remember that it's just a machine. My serger sometimes gets a little cranky. This can result in me getting a little cranky as well, especially when trying to meet a deadline. Many of us sew to change our pace and get away from the stress of daily life. Don't let this machine stress you out. Take some deep breaths, stretch, and get something refreshing to drink. Then do basic troubleshooting. Rethread, reset the tensions, change the needles, and try again.

Selecting a Garment to Embellish

As a general rule, I don't design garment patterns. In response to the demands of my students for more serger classes on garment embellishments, I started to adapt creative serger techniques to embellish garment patterns currently on the market. There are so many wonderful patterns to choose from.

It doesn't matter what kind of garment you use as a canvas for your wearable art. The serger can be used to embellish any kind of project. You are only limited by your imagination. You can create wearable art from scratch using the pattern of your choice to construct the entire garment, including embellishments. Plan the embellishments for your garments to incorporate the many quick and easy techniques that can be done on a serger.

It's always easier to embellish a flat pattern without darts but most women have curves. We often need more shape to our garments than can be achieved with a no-darts pattern. For class projects, I usually recommend a pattern without darts so students can spend the class time working with serger techniques instead of dealing with fitting and design issues. But each individual should decide what pattern to use for their garment. Select patterns for your wearable art that are suited to your lifestyle and will coordinate with other garments in your wardrobe.

The process is faster if the pattern has fairly simple lines without a lot of small pattern pieces. However, if you decide to use a pattern with many pieces, design the embellishments to fit within the shape of each pattern piece. A garment with many pattern pieces will require more planning for the placement of the embellishments.

If you don't always have time to create and embellish an entire garment from scratch, consider using ready-made garments as your canvas. There are many serger embellishments that can be applied to your already existing wardrobe. It's not considered cheating to use the time you have available to make embellishments rather than construct from scratch.

In my classes, everyone is encouraged to select a pattern that reflects their own style. This allows each person to make what they want instead of exactly duplicating a sample garment. Everyone uses the same basic serger techniques, but all the garments are unique creations.

My teaching attitude is reflected in this book. You can follow exact project instructions and re-create the sample garment or you can follow the technique instructions and design the SergeArt placement on the garment pattern of your choice. For those of you just venturing into the field of wearable art, it's often better to duplicate the sample garment the first time you experiment with new techniques. This lets you focus on the creative serging techniques instead of the garment design aspects.

Style & Fit

Often people spend many hours creating a beautifully-crafted garment only to leave it hanging in the closet because they dislike the basic garment style or the way it fits.

There are many great books available to help you determine your body type. They give recommendations for specific styles to wear that are flattering for every different body type (see the Bibliography). It's extremely important to like the way your

garments look and fit. With all the information available, there is no reason why you shouldn't be able to make a garment that enhances your shape and fits you well. It doesn't matter what size or shape you are. It is well worth the time to find a flattering, well-fitting style for your shape.

I have observed that many people expect to buy a pattern in their size, cut it out, sew it, and wear it, without ever taking a single measurement. A good fit can happen by accident this way, but this won't be the case for most people. There are several fitting issues to deal with before beginning to cut fabric for the garment. Some folks will settle for a less than perfect fit from ready-to-wear but expect a pattern to fit with no effort made at measuring themselves and the pattern first. Spend the time to customize the fit of your basic patterns.

If you are happy with the way your garment looks and fits, the results of your creative efforts won't be left hanging in the back of a closet.

Altering the Pattern

Many students have told me of cutting and making a garment straight from a pattern, then having to find someone else it will fit. Patterns are designed to fit ideal body proportions. Size measurements are not standard for all pattern designers. They cannot take into account that your arms may be 3" longer than mine even though we wear the same size. I have to shorten all sleeves to obtain a decent fit from a pattern. I have narrow shoulders and must cut the shoulder area in a smaller size to prevent the shoulder seams from hanging to my elbows. These fitting issues are taken into consideration when buying new patterns. I always buy multi-sized patterns.

Tracing a copy from a multi-sized master pattern allows me to use different sizes in the areas where needed. By blending the cutting lines, no one ever knows my garment is actually a combination of several different sizes. I always make a new pattern from muslin before spending time making a garment that won't fit. Take the time to make a muslin garment from the pattern to ensure that it fits.

There are many books on fitting and pattern making available to help you fine tune any fitting issues (see the Bibliography). Take a fitting class or watch videos for additional information that will help you in this area.

Using Patterns More than Once

Pick some classic garment styles based on your body type, fine tune the fit, and reuse the patterns. By using different fabric, trim, and techniques, the garments won't look like duplicates of the same pattern.

Many patterns are suitable for cutting into sections and it's really very easy to do. Make a copy of the original and draw lines to divide it into sections. Add seam allowances to both sides of the cutting lines and the sections will fit back together when sewn. You can also overlap the sections on a base fabric that has been cut from the intact pattern and cover the raw edges with a trim or serged strip of fabric.

There are some great books (see the Bibliography) available on how to make basic design changes to get the most mileage from your favorite patterns. Shirley Adams, on her PBS program *The Sewing Connection*, shares a great deal of information on how to make basic changes to a pattern to achieve many different looks.

The Basic Wardrobe

- *Long Vest*
- *Short Vest*
- *Blazer Jacket*
- *Casual Jacket*
- *Pullover Blouse*
- *Button Up Blouse*

These are some basic patterns for creating a wearable art wardrobe. You can vary the look by changing the neckline, sleeve length, and hem length. Add or remove lapels on the jacket. Try an asymmetrical look by changing the basic shape of the pattern pieces. Vary the location of the front closures when reusing a pattern. If you embellish each garment differently, you will get a lot more use from your patterns and you won't have to make a muslin of every garment because you will have already made changes to the pattern pieces. Many types of embellishments are compatible with these basic garment styles.

Types of Fabric for SergeArt

The garments featured in this book are made from 100% cotton fabrics. Cotton is my all-time favorite fabric to sew and

wear, although many different kinds of fabric can be used when making wearable art.

Choose fabrics for garments and embellishments that are fairly compatible and require the same cleaning methods. Prewash all fabrics to prevent any surprises from happening when cleaning the garments. I always serge the cut edges of fabric before prewashing to prevent raveling in the washer and dryer. This also lets me know the fabric has already been washed.

If using fabrics of different weights, press iron-on knit interfacing to the wrong side of the lighter one to equalize the weight. Knit interfacing won't stiffen the fabric and is my favorite interfacing to use for wearable art garments.

Determining Yardage

Since you are using patterns of your choice, you will determine the amount of fabric needed to create your garment. Suggestions are included to help determine the amount of yardage needed. All yardages given for garments are only recommendations. Actual yardage will vary, depending on the style and size of the pattern used. The only way to determine yardage is to measure the pattern pieces.

The lining and underlining yardage can be determined from amounts indicated on the pattern.

Feel free to use as many fabrics as you want in your garments. Many of these techniques are a good way to use up small amounts of fabric.

Also measure the pattern pieces to determine yardage needed for embellishments. Measure the pattern pieces before cutting any fabric for the embellishments. Measure the length and width of any section to be embellished and make the finished fabric several inches larger than the exact size needed. You can minimize the amount of wasted fabric and decorative thread when creating wearable art by making only what you need.

When cutting strips of fabric, add seam allowances to each side of the strip. This amount should be added to the total yardage.

Draw new pattern shapes from the original pattern. When you cut a pattern into sections, add seam allowances where the sections need to overlap.

It may seem like a lot of extra work to measure pattern pieces and figure some basic math, but the end results are well worth the time.

Underlining
(Base Fabric)

The underlining replaces interfacing and helps the garment maintain its shape. This inner layer of fabric removes the stress from the embellished fabric and increases the life of the garment.

Cut the underlining of the garment from prewashed muslin or cotton fabric. The underlining is also the base fabric for the embellishments. The embellished fabric sections are stitched to the underlining and then handled as one layer.

Some embellishments contain several layers of fabric and will cause the finished garment to hang off-balance. The use of thick decorative thread also adds weight. Use extra layers of underlining fabric to add weight where needed to balance the drape of the garment.

Cutting & Sewing the Pattern

Sewing is like putting together a jigsaw puzzle. The pieces fit together to make a whole. Accurate cutting and sewing are key to making the pieces fit. You can sew the seams together evenly but if the pieces aren't cut right, they won't fit together smoothly. Conversely, if you cut the pieces accurately but the sewing is crooked and wanders down the seamline, the finished product will be crooked and warped no matter how accurately it is cut.

When cutting the embellished fabric one layer at a time, don't forget to flip the pattern piece over when cutting the second time so you will have a left and right side. You can also trace two copies of the same pattern, but be sure to mark them left and right. Draw all the placement and grain lines right on the pattern. For a pattern piece cut on a fold, place the pattern on the folded edge of a large piece of tracing paper, trace, and cut out the pattern.

Cutting Fabric Strips
For Embellishments

All the strips used for embellishments are cut across the grain, from selvage to selvage. The fabrics you use may vary from 40" to 60" in width. For example, the instructions may say to cut a strip 3" x 44". This means to cut a 3"-wide strip across

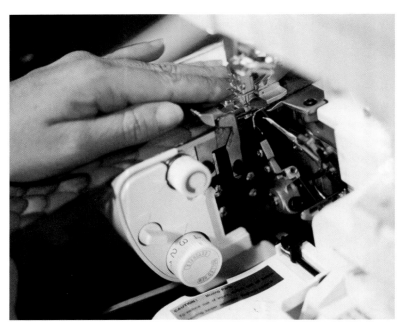

Don't cut any fabric off the strips with the serger.

the fabric from selvage to selvage. The 44" length is just used for consistency.

The best way to achieve accuracy when cutting is to use a rotary cutter and ruler. Don't cut any fabric from the strips while serging. It will affect the size of the finished piece of fabric.

Embellishment Seams & Seam Allowances

When you have embellished sections to be stitched to a base fabric, always add a seam allowance to the edges that will be against another section. All embellished sections should overlap each other to help distribute the stress placed on the garment sections during normal wear.

Always add in seam allowances when figuring the yardage needed for pieced embellishments. Many techniques will require extra yardage due to the number of seam allowances.

Don't cut anything off when serging strips together to create embellished fabric. If the trimming isn't even, ripples will be created in the finished fabric and it won't lay flat. This distortion will be especially pronounced when uneven amounts are cut off the strips as you serge. The fabric can often be salvaged if it distorts, but not always.

A serger doesn't sew as precisely as a sewing machine. The seams are bulky when using decorative thread and it takes some effort to get the seams to match. Sometimes they won't line up exactly no matter what you do. Take this into account when planning your embellishments. You can avoid having to match the seams by placing a solid strip between pieced strips or staggering the seams.

Garment Seams & Seam Allowances

For final garment construction on the sewing machine, use the seam allowance recommended in the pattern instructions - usually 1/4" to 5/8". However, on a serger 5/8" seams are cumbersome to handle. Most people worry about evenly cutting the excess seam allowance away, or worse, cutting too much fabric off. There is an easy way to solve the problem. Trace patterns with a 3/8" seam allowance. Just skim the edges of the fabric with the knife while serging to keep the layers even (cut less than 1/8"). This is much easier than trying to figure out, while serging around various garment shapes, how much to evenly cut away the 5/8" seam allowance.

Incorporating these Techniques in Other Projects

When deciding on the placement for your embellishments, it is often better to go asymmetrical rather than try to get everything to match. Decorative seams are thick and when stacked they will usually shift a little when serged. It's better to plan nonmatching seams in the design than to be dissatisfied with slightly offset seams.

Always consider the amount of wear an area will have. There is also the snag-ability factor to consider when planning where to place your serger embellishments. Some serger stitches are more likely to snag when placed in areas of wear or friction. I don't put many serger embellishments on the sleeves because that's the most likely place to get snagged carrying a purse or other items on my shoulder. For example, a flatlock stitch snags more easily than a rolled edge and the loop side of a flatlock stitch snags more easily than the ladder side.

Final Garment Construction

Final garment construction can be done on the serger, sewing machine, or a combination of both. Several of the patterns used for garments in this book are constructed with both machines. I sew everything possible with the serger except when techniques are better suited to the sewing machine.

The way some patterns are designed makes some construction techniques better done on a sewing machine. In this case, serge the raw edges of the fabric pieces without cutting away the seam allowance before sewing the seams together.

Many garments can be totally constructed on the serger. Instructions are included in Chapter 4 for constructing a vest entirely on the serger. It's best to trim the excess seam allowances from the pattern before cutting the fabric. Serge the seams together without trimming any fabric.

I don't always follow the final construction instructions recommended by the pattern designer. Choose the final construction method best suited to the types of embellishments used.

Perfectionism

The biggest obstacle to creativity I have observed through many years of teaching is the tendency toward perfectionism. A symptom of this is the inability to start something for fear of a less than perfect result. It may take forever to start a project and it may never get finished. As a recovering perfectionist, I can definitely relate to the issue. In every one of my classes at least one person, sometimes more, suffers from this malady. Please don't beat yourself up over this one. Life is tough enough without being your own worst enemy.

Perfectionism can be a good thing up to a point but shouldn't interfere with getting things accomplished. My advice on this subject is to strive to get over it! Seeking perfection is sometimes debilitating and usually self-defeating. You may slip from time to time, but that is far better than dealing with the constant unattainable desire for perfection.

Artists and craftspeople from all parts of the globe have

long-standing customs of intentionally adding a flaw to their creations. This is to insure they don't get caught up in the self-defeating aspects of seeking perfection. Life is too short to agonize over the small stuff. Once you achieve perfection, what else is there to strive for?

Surrender to the idea of being able to let anything happen. If you end up with something different from the expected results, view it as an opportunity to stretch your mind for a creative solution.

Have a Road Map for Your Creative Journey (But Be Willing to Detour Or Ask Directions)

Make a plan and have an idea of where you're going. It's like having a map to follow to your destination. You can always change your mind and go a different direction, but you at least have an idea of where you want to go. Pick a project, take a deep breath, and do it!

I don't always end up with the exact garment I started out to make. My sketches and notes may get changed throughout the project. Things usually change and develop as I make them. Most often I start with a stack of extremely colorful fabrics and threads, then figure out what can be done with them.

My Granny used to tell me that it was usually best to leave well enough alone. I try to keep that comment in the back of my mind when making a garment. I always think of things I could do differently or better. However, Granny's advice wins out and those differences are applied to the next project. Many garments in this book are a result of this approach.

Mistakes Are a Great Source For Inspiration

Some of the most wonderfully creative ideas result from covering up mistakes and accidents. Mistakes happen. I can guarantee it. I really enjoy the challenge of helping people find creative ways to deal with accidents or just flat-out backward sewing. View your mistakes as an opportunity for more creativity.

Always be willing to try a different and possibly better method of sewing. Don't ever let the fear of making a mistake or of having your garment look different from the sample keep you from trying something totally new and different from what you are comfortable doing.

The beautiful jacket in this photo was almost abandoned before completion. All the pleated fabric was created and ready to cut for final garment construction, but in the process of cutting the jacket fronts from the pleated fabric, the pattern piece wasn't flipped over to cut the second side. What do you do with two fronts that go on the same side? This left a couple of options - either make a new piece of pleated fabric or figure out a creative way to use the miscut front. Since there wasn't enough fabric or time to make a new piece of pleated fabric, the only choice was to creatively fix the mistake. After some brainstorming, the solution was to use the leftover Seminole patchwork from the shoulder yoke and piece it to the front of the jacket to fill in the missing pleated fabric. Would you have known this had happened by looking at the finished jacket?

Peek-a-Boo Pleats Jacket made by Jo Largent, Houston.

24

CHAPTER 2

*Notions &
Accessories
for the Creative Serger*

I love to use notions and gadgets. They are extremely helpful to achieve faster, better, and more accurate results. The notions listed are recommended for the projects in this book. They are available through your local fabric retailer or mail order source.

Notions for Threading & Using Decorative Threads

ThreadPRO

ThreadPRO is a unique thread delivery system. It is a stand designed to minimize thread twisting and breakage and can lubricate the thread before it is delivered to the machine. It is especially useful with metallic and other specialty threads and can also handle heavy commercial cones of thread.

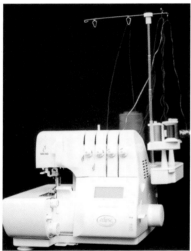

Mixing different types of thread is much easier when using the proper notions.

Tweezers

Tweezers are a necessity when threading a serger. Sergers come with tweezers in the accessory kits but the quality varies from brand to brand. If you are not comfortable with the tweezers that came with your serger, upgrade to a better pair. Make sure your tweezers can grab and hold threads. Tweezers that grip only on the tips are harder to manipulate; you want a pair with a larger gripping surface. A hemostat makes a great pair of serger tweezers.

Looper & Needle Threaders

Some serger accessory kits include looper and needle threaders. There are several types of looper threaders available from your dealer or favorite mail order source to assist you when using decorative threads. Dental floss threaders work wonderfully for threading the loopers of your serger. Needle threaders have a loop of wire thin enough to fit through the eye. Many new sergers have needle threaders built in.

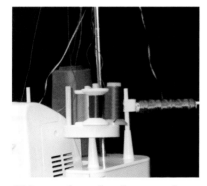

Using a thread palette and a horizontal spool pin.

Horizontal Spool Pin

This notion fits on the thread spindle and can accommodate different size spools of thread. It is indispensable when using metallics, ribbon floss, and other decorative threads. Many threads are not meant to feed upward from the end of the spool. They will twist, knot, and break. Use a horizontal spool pin so the thread spool can freely rotate, allowing the thread to feed evenly without twisting.

Thread Nets

Many sergers come with these in the accessory kit. Thread nets are very useful when using slippery types of thread. Using a thread net increases the amount of tension on your thread and you may need to adjust your tension to compensate.

Thread Palette

This notion fits over the thread spindle and has four mini spindles that allow you to blend up to five regular sized spools of thread at a time through a single looper or up to two through a single needle. This is for decorative serging and you can blend several specialty threads to make beautiful embellishments. When using metallic threads on your thread palette you can also use horizontal spool pins to keep the metallics from twisting.

E-Z Winder

This notion works on the bobbin winder on your sewing machine. It allows you to wind many types of threads onto spools. The package contains four empty spools and the adapter that fits on the bobbin winder of the sewing machine. You can also purchase additional empty spools. This is great when you want to use crochet thread, yarn, ribbons, etc. You can buy one large spool of thread and wind it onto smaller spools instead of having to purchase a separate cone of thread for each position. There are also several brands of thread that have spools that will fit on the winder. Save empty spools that fit on the adapter.

Notions to Aid in Serging

Tilt'able Sewing Platforms

This is an angled platform made to fit under sewing machines and sergers. It tilts the machine toward you, making it easier to see the work area without having to crane your neck. It vastly improves your posture while sewing and reduces neck, shoulder, and back strain. As one who has had many neck and back problems, I highly recommend this product and won't sew or serge without one. I can't stress enough the importance of correct posture to make the sewing experience more enjoyable. This is the most advantageous product I can recommend to promote happy and healthy serging.

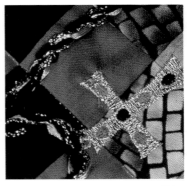

Clear Acrylic Extension Tables

These portable acrylic tables provide a flatbed surface for your serger. This helps you feed the fabric more smoothly and greatly improves your posture while serging because it supports the weight of the fabric. These tables can be used on a flat surface or can be tilted to work with a tilted sewing platform.

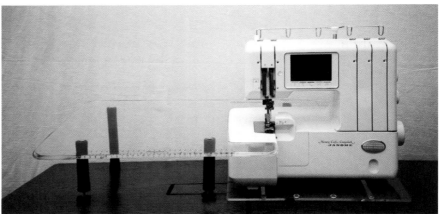

Needles

Many sergers use regular sewing machine needles; some use industrial needles. Check your manual for the correct needle for your brand of serger and always follow those recommendations. Always have extra needles on hand.

It's also important to use the correct size and type of needle for the fabric. Your serger manual has a chart to suggest what size and type of needle to use in your serger for different types and weights of fabric. The most common size needles to use in sergers are 11/75, 12/80, and 90/14. Universal needles size 11/75 or 12/80 are recommended for the garments in this book. An embroidery or topstitching needle is used for the Ultra Crazypatch Vest.

Dull or bent needles can cause skipped stitches, thread breakage, tension problems, and damage to the fabric. Needles should be changed frequently to insure the best stitch quality. Change your needles after approximately eight hours of serging (or every three garments) and more often if sewing on heavyweight fabrics. Change needles more often if you do a lot of serging on each project. Bad needles cause bad problems! Changing needles often is the best stress reducer there is when serging. Many serger problems can be solved just by using a new needle.

Seam Ripper

As ye sew, so shall ye rip. This is a necessity for the "frog stitch" (ripit, ripit, ripit), also called reverse sewing. A seam ripper is the most useful notion to have. There are several types of seam rippers available designed specifically to remove serger stitches. Replace your seam ripper when it gets dull.

Seam Sealant

There are many brands of seam sealants available. Use your favorite brand to seal and help prevent fraying of the end of your serged seams. Some brands stiffen when dry and are a bit scratchy so don't use them on areas that will directly touch the skin. I prefer the brands that are soft to the touch when dry.

Notions to Aid in Making Embellished Fabric

Stabilizers

There are many types and brands of stabilizers useful in creating wearable art. Sulky of America makes stabilizers for any need you might have: stick-on, iron-on, tear-off, cut-away, heat-away, etc. They have published a great book on stabilizers that answers any questions on what, when, where, why, and how to use to use them (see the Bibliography).

Photo courtesy of Sulky of America.

Rotary Cutter, Cutting Mat, Rulers, and Weights

I can't live without these items. They really speed up the cutting process. There are many different brands of these products available. Measurements and cuts are much more exact than when cutting with scissors.

Rotary cutters look like pizza cutters with one exception - a round razor blade that is extremely sharp. There are several types and sizes of rotary cutters. Some are curved to fit the hand. There are some that close by themselves. Train yourself to

always close a rotary cutter before laying it down. There are sharpeners available to resharpen the blade when it gets dull.

A cutting mat is necessary to keep from cutting the surface under the fabric with the blade. Most mats have a numbered grid to use for measuring. I prefer Omnigrid mats and rulers. The rulers have markings you can see on any color of fabric. The mats have measurement lines that extend past the borders with the numbers on all four sides instead of just two. This makes it much easier to line up the ruler.

Rulers come in all shapes and sizes - squares, rectangles, triangles, wedges, in sizes that are narrow, wide, long, and short. Quilting shops usually carry a wide variety of rulers in many different shapes.

To keep from having to pin the pattern to the fabric when cutting, use pattern weights. Huge metal washers from the hardware store make great, inexpensive pattern weights.

Iron

An iron is a necessary part of any sewing room (or corner). There are many brands of irons to choose from. Steam and heat are the main requirements. I may not iron my clothes often after they're made, but every seam gets pressed as I'm making it.

Press Cloth

Cheesecloth is most often used for a press cloth. You can buy press cloths in a package at your local sewing retailer or use a lightweight piece of white fabric. Some threads melt from the heat of an iron. Some fabrics (such as Ultrasuede) can be permanently marked by using an iron on the face of the fabric. There's nothing worse than completing your garment and then ruining it by not using a press cloth when pressing.

Iron-On Knit Interfacing

There are many brands of iron-on knit interfacing available in a variety of widths. Knit interfacing has a soft drape and won't add bulk to your garments. I used it in several of the featured garments. It's best to buy this in four to five yard lengths so you will have plenty on hand.

T-Pins and Bodkins

These are used for creating the woven fabrics. Use T-pins to anchor fabric strips to the weaving board. A bodkin attached to the end of the strip will aid in pulling the strips through to weave the fabric.

Weaving Board

This is indispensable when weaving fabric. It allows you to pin the strips securely in a vertical or lengthwise direction (warp) while weaving strips through from the horizontal direction (weft). When the weaving is complete, you can press it to an iron-on interfacing while it is still pinned in place.

You can purchase a ready-made weaving board from your favorite retailer or mail order source or you can make your own by covering one side of several layers of thick cardboard tightly with a towel or cotton quilt batting and fabric.

To make a long-lasting and sturdy ironing/weaving board, start with a piece of 1/4" plywood cut to the desired size. I have one 24" x 36" for large projects and one 24" x 24" for smaller projects. Cover the board with a layer of batting, then fabric. I used the wrong side of a black and white striped fabric to cover mine (the wrong side tones down the contrast of the colors and the stripes aid in lining up the weaving strips and getting everything squared up). Use a stapler to attach everything to the back of the board (I used a regular desk stapler).

Just lay the board right on top of an ironing board or table to use it. Use T-pins to hold the strips for weaving projects. They stick into the wood far enough to hold the project down quite well. Straight pins will work in cardboard.

If using polyester batting instead of cotton, it may be too thick. Most polyester battings will separate into two layers. Cut the batting the size needed and then peel it apart into two layers and use only one layer to cover the board.

Feet & Other Serger Accessories

I admit, I am a foot-aholic. I have every kind of foot there is for all my machines. It's difficult to do certain techniques without the right kind of foot. Serger feet and accessories are not often interchangeable between brands, so buy accessories that are specific to your serger. Make sure the foot you purchase is for the intended use. Some feet may be called by different names, depending on the brand.

Following are the feet used for techniques in the featured garments.

Fabric or Seam Guide

This accessory attaches to the serger and guides the fabric so the knife won't cut it. Some sergers come with a guide or as an extra accessory. There are other brands that don't make them at all. Check your manual or with your dealer.

Blind Hem Foot

This foot has an adjustable fabric guide. Adjust it to the left side and it keeps the folded edge of the fabric lined up with the needle to make a blind hem. Adjust it to the right side to get the widest stitch width and to keep the fabric from being cut by the blade. Be sure to check your manual for the correct needle position to use with the blind hem foot. Many sergers have blind hem feet that will only let you use the right needle position, which gives you a much narrower stitch width. Most brands have this foot available.

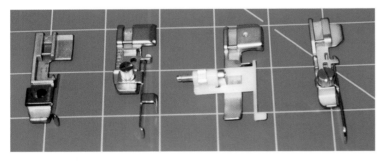

Blind hem feet have adjustable fabric guides.

Rolled Hem Foot

Some brands have a separate rolled hem foot that comes with the machine. Other brands use the same all-purpose foot for rolled hemming and standard serging. Refer to your manual for the specifics for your serger.

Piping Foot

This foot is available for most sergers. It has a groove in the bottom of the foot for the piping cord to fit in. This keeps the piping nice and even as it is being made or inserted with the serger. This foot can be used to insert zippers because the teeth can run through the groove.

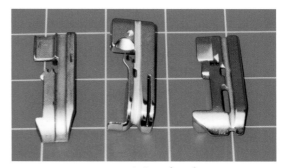

Piping feet have a groove on the bottom.

Shirring or Gathering Foot

This is a weird looking foot but it is my favorite one to use. The shirring foot will gather and attach one layer of fabric to another layer that stays flat. It has a separator blade on the bottom to cover the feed dogs and prevent the differential feed from gathering it. The layer of fabric to be gathered is placed under the separator and the fabric that stays flat is placed in the slot above it. You must have differential feed for this foot to work. Refer to the differential feed information on page 38 to learn more about the settings to use.

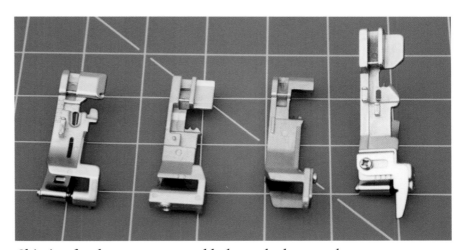

Shirring feet have a separator blade on the bottom that prevents one layer of fabric from gathering.

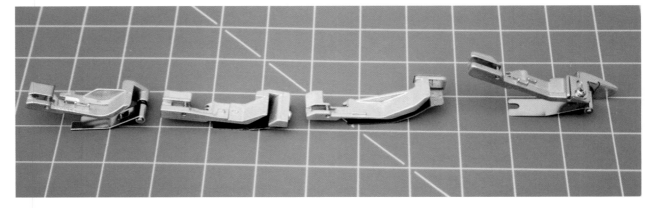

Side view showing the separator blade of the shirring foot.

CHAPTER 3

Serger & Basics Guidelines

You must experiment and practice to get the most out of your serger. Play with the tensions to see what the results are with various settings. You may come up with a new stitch!

It's important to learn the parts of your serger and what they do. The generic serger in this chapter provides the basic features. Study the detailed picture in your serger manual until you're familiar with the features on your machine. It's very beneficial to attend serger classes.

There are many practical as well as decorative techniques that can be done on your serger. Brands and models of sergers vary in capability but you will be able to do many, if not all, of the techniques in this book. The projects in this book are geared toward three/four thread sergers since they are the most popular models.

The Flatlocked Lapel Coat (page121) is embellished on the collar with the two-thread

Generic Serger

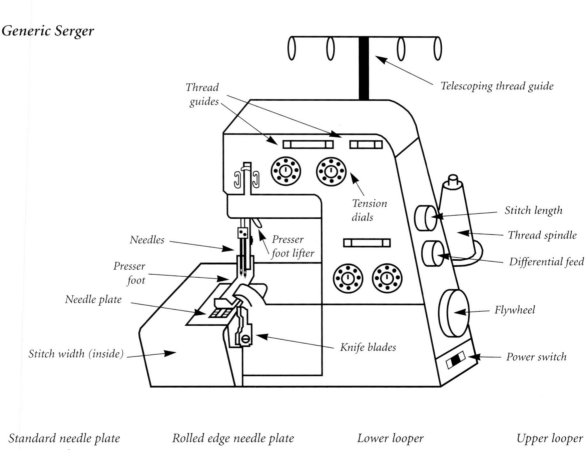

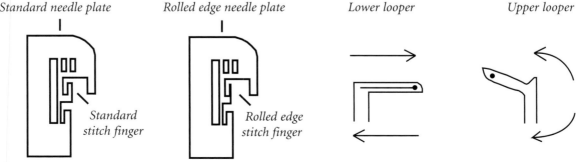

chain stitch only available on five-thread sergers. Older models of five-thread sergers aren't able to stitch in the middle of the fabric so you must be able to disengage the upper looper and have a flatbed extension table to cover the knife area. Most five-thread sergers made in the last few years have this stitch capability.

There are some three-thread techniques that can be done with two threads if your serger has that capability. Refer to your manual to see if your serger is designed for conversion to two threads. The needle and lower looper are used for this stitch.

A stitch setting chart has been included in Chapter 5 for you to copy. Make samples of the stitches and pin them to the page with the settings. Be sure to write down your settings, types of thread used, and any special instructions that apply to your serger.

Allow yourself time and practice to master these techniques. Your samples may not be perfect and that's okay. Be kind to yourself - Rome wasn't built in a day.

Parts of the Serger

The best way to master a serger is to understand how it operates. You adjust for different stitches by changing the settings of the tensions, length, and width. It's important to know where these controls are and what they do. Familiarize yourself with the terminology. Your manual should have all the information you need to set up your serger to do any of the techniques in this book.

Study the pictures and diagrams in your manual until you are comfortable with your serger. There are differences between brands and even models of the same brand of sergers. It's not possible to give you the specific tension settings for each technique. Your serger manual will give the recommended settings to use for your particular brand. The only place to find recommended settings for your model is in the manual or book specific to your brand of serger.

Find marks on the foot or plate that you can use to help you guide the fabric where you want it. Many sergers have markings on the foot that line up with the needles.

Following are the features of a serger you should be familiar with. Please refer to your manual as you cover these topics to learn the specifics of your serger.

Needle Plate

This is a metal plate that attaches to the bed of the serger. Some sergers require that you change the needle plate for regular or rolled hem serging. Other models have a multi-purpose needle plate and the stitch finger is on the foot or totally separate. It's important to remove the needle plate occasionally and thoroughly clean the lint from underneath it.

Stitch Finger

This small metal prong attached to the needle plate determines the stitch width. Some sergers have stitch fingers attached to the feet. The stitch finger on the foot determines the width of the stitch. Other models have a separate stitch finger that slides in and out of place for regular or rolled edge stitching. Or you may have a stitch finger that has to be totally removed to make a rolled edge. The serger stitches are actually formed around the stitch finger, then laid on the fabric. The rolled hem stitch finger is about the diameter of a hand-sewing needle.

Stitch Width

The stitch width is the distance between the needle stitch line and the edge of the fabric. Some sergers have no stitch width control dial. The width is determined by using either the left or right needle. Most models, however, do have a stitch width control dial that allows you to adjust to a specific width. The stitch width control moves the fixed blade to determine the width. Stitch widths range from 1 mm to 7 mm. Refer to your manual to find the stitch width control. Your manual will give the range of widths for your serger and how to change them. On some models, the stitch finger is built into the foot and this controls the width. A dramatic change in width will usually require making tension adjustments. Use a wide stitch for serging medium to heavy fabrics and decorative serging and a narrow width for rolled hems and lightweight fabrics.

The needle plate on the left has a single rolled hem stitch finger. The one on the right is for wider stitching.

The stitch width control is found near the needle plate area.

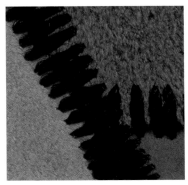

Stitch length, differential feed, and speed controls.

Stitch Length

All sergers have a stitch length control. Stitch length is the distance from one needle stitch to another. Stitch lengths range from 0.5 mm to 5 mm. Refer to your manual to find the stitch length control. The average stitch length used for most construction serging is 2½ mm to 3 mm. For a satin stitch, set the length to 1 mm (or a little less on some machines). Don't set the length too close for thick thread or it can build up on the stitch finger and cause a jam.

Differential Feed & Feed Dogs

The feed dog is under the presser foot and has metal teeth that come up through the needle plate to grip the fabric and move it through the serger. The amount of movement is controlled by the stitch length setting. The feed dog extends past the front edge of the presser foot and will pull the fabric under the foot without having to manually raise it with the presser foot lifter. There is only one feed dog on sergers without differential feed.

Differential feed means there are two feed dogs that can be adjusted to different feeding ratios. The differential feed ratio ranges from 0.5 to 2. A setting of 1 (or N on some brands) gives you even feeding with both feed dogs moving at the same ratio. Use this setting for normal serging.

When you engage the differential feed and set the ratio anywhere between 1 and 2, the front feed dog will pull in more fabric than the back one. This causes the fabric to gather or ease, depending on the setting used. Use this setting with a shirring foot or to keep fabrics from stretching while being serged.

When you engage the differential feed and set the ratio anywhere below 1, the front feed dog will pull in less fabric than the back one. This causes the fabric to stretch. This setting reduces puckers when putting seams in lightweight fabrics.

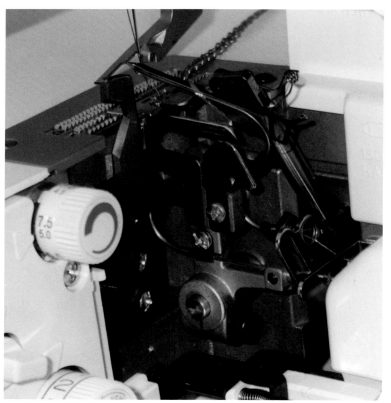

Feed dog and looper area with foot removed for visibility.

Cutting Blades (Knives)

Sergers have a movable blade and a stationary blade. The two blades are located in front of the needles and to the right of the foot on all serger models. The blades trim the fabric before the fabric is stitched. There are several different types of cutting systems. Some blades drop down from the top while others come from beneath the needle plate. When you don't want to cut, the blades can be moved out of the way or disengaged by being locked in place. Always fully disengage the knife if not using it for cutting.

Needle Positions

With the variety of stitch combinations available on today's sergers, I won't go into all the possible combinations available to you. Refer to your manual to become familiar with this information. The projects in this book use the left, right, or chain stitch needle positions. Use the left needle position for a wide stitch and the right needle position for a narrow stitch. Make sure the needles are properly inserted.

Upper & Lower Loopers

Loopers are moving metal fingers with a hole or "eye" at the tip to carry thread that is wrapped around the edge of the fabric and is locked in place by the needle thread (hence the term overlocker). The upper looper moves up over the needle plate and down beside it in a half circle direction and lays thread on the top of the fabric. The lower looper moves from side to side under the needle plate and lays thread on the bottom of the fabric. The looper threads interlock at the edge of the fabric. The large size of the eye allows you to use many types of decorative thread in the loopers. It's important to thread the loopers in the correct order. Refer to your manual for specifics.

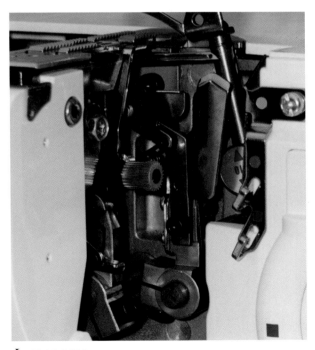

Looper area.

Chain Stitch Looper

The chain stitch looper is only found on five-thread sergers. It's situated in front of the lower looper and moves from side to side under the needle plate. It interlocks with the chain stitch needle thread and makes a removable chain of thread on the bottom of the fabric. The large size of the eye allows you to use many types of decorative thread.

Tension Dials & Adjustments

Your machine may have two, three, four, or five different thread positions - left needle, right needle, upper looper, lower looper, chain stitch needle, and chain stitch looper. There is a tension control to correspond to each thread position. The higher the number, the tighter the tension.

There are wrap-around dials, drop-in dials, and now there are computerized sergers with no tension control dials at all.

Serging on different weights of fabric may require that you make slight tension adjustments. The extra thickness of the fabric will cause the stitches to be too tight and the lighter weight of the fabric will make the stitches too loose.

Changing the stitch width will have an effect on the tension adjustment. If you make the stitch wider, you may have to loosen the tension to allow for the extra space created by using a wider stitch. If you narrow the stitch, you may have to tighten the tension to take up the slack in the thread created by the narrower width.

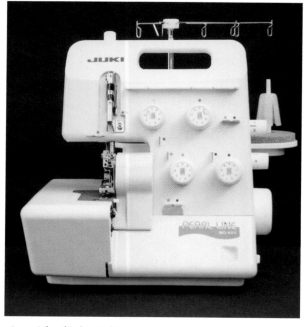

Outside dials, Juki.

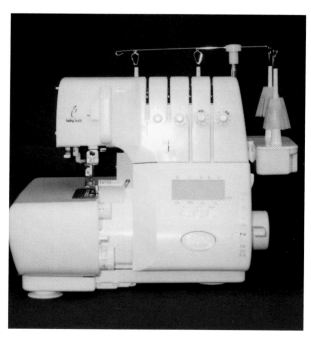

Drop in tension dials, Babylock.

The same holds true if you change the stitch length. By lengthening the stitch, the tension becomes too tight. There isn't enough thread to travel the extra distance between stitches so you will need to loosen the tension. Shortening the stitch causes the tension to be too loose. Since there is less distance

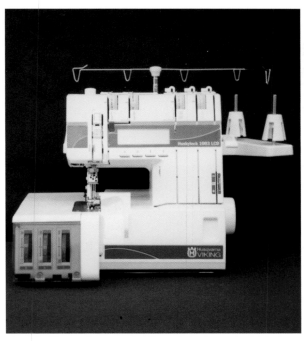

Drop in tension dials, Viking.

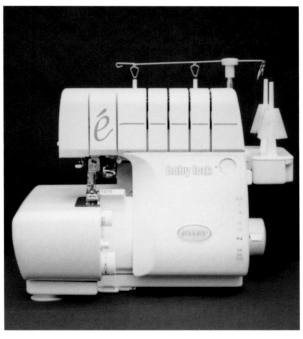

No tension dials, Babylock.

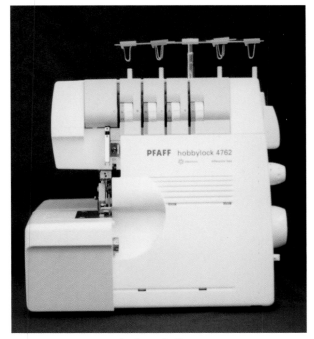

Drop in tension dials, Pfaff.

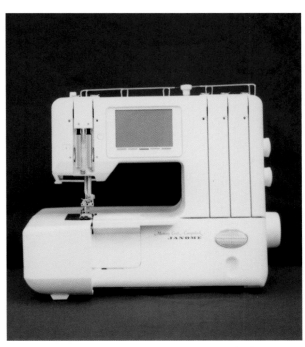

Computerized touch screen tension dials, Janome.

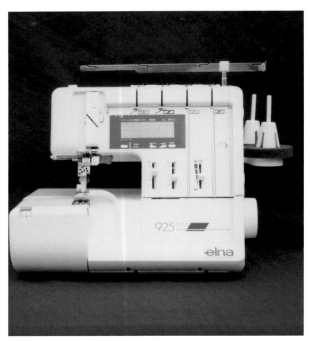
Computerized push button tension dials, Elna.

between the stitches, you will have to tighten the tension to take up the slack.

Remember the relationship between fabric weight, stitch length, and width to tension adjustment and it will make tension adjustment a lot easier.

General Guidelines For Serging

Here are some general guidelines to follow when using a serger. These guidelines are not arranged in any order of importance because they're all equally important. Refer to them often until they become ingrained serger habits. Most serger habits are different from sewing machine habits so be patient with yourself as you learn them.

Threading

Release the tension or loosen the tensions all the way when threading. This allows the thread to properly seat itself between the tension disks. Reset the tensions after threading is complete. You have to turn those dials! Some sergers have a tension release and don't need to be reset manually.

If you tie on to rethread, don't sew the knots through your machine. Reduce the tensions all the way and pull one or all the threads through the guides by hand. Use the tweezers and grip the thread behind the looper eye to pull one thread through at a time. Unthread the needle eyes before pulling the thread through so you don't bend the needles! Rethread the needles when the new thread is in place.

Always thread a serger in the correct order. Refer to your manual for the correct sequence. This is an important step and helps reduce the chance of trapping the threads. Make sure to become familiar with the threading order for your serger.

If the lower looper thread breaks, always unwrap the needle threads from around the lower looper before rethreading it. If you don't, the needle thread will be trapped. When the needle is first threaded, the thread goes through the eye and straight back. As the first stitch is made, the needle thread goes under the needle plate and is caught by the lower looper. This causes the needle thread to be wrapped around the lower looper from front to back where it goes back up through the needle plate and joins the thread chain. If you thread the lower looper from scratch and leave the needle threads wrapped around the lower looper, the needle threads will be trapped between the lower looper and the lower looper thread. This will cause the lower looper thread to break repeatedly until you rethread the needles or remove the needle thread from around the lower looper. Look inside your serger when it is properly threaded and making a chain to see the needle thread wrapped around the lower looper.

Needles

Needles should be changed frequently to insure the best stitch quality. Dull or bent needles can cause skipped stitches, thread breakage, tension problems, and damage to the fabric. Some of the most common problems that occur when serging are caused by using old or damaged needles. People spend frustrating hours trying to adjust and/or "fix" their serger when all they need to do is change the needles! This would have given them a lot of extra time to accomplish something else. Sewing has been proven to be beneficial and reduce stress but only if you put new needles in your serger when needed.

Serging

Always test serge on a piece of the fabric you will be using. Before starting a project, make all the necessary tension, length, and width adjustments using the same fabric and number of layers that you will be serging.

Always leave a 4" chain of thread behind the foot. This will help prevent the thread from jamming the next time you start serging. It helps to hold the chain with your fingertips as you start serging the first few stitches.

Sit down at your serger. Raise the presser foot, then tap on the foot pedal while watching the chain of thread at the same time. See how the thread jumps? That's what usually causes a tangled mess that forces you to rethread. If you hold the thread chain by just laying a couple of fingers on it when you first start to serge, the speed of the machine won't yank the threads

back into the loopers and get tangled. You can also get a tangle if the chain is cut too short. It will jump forward when the serger starts and get in the way of the new stitches that are being formed.

Keep an eye on what the stitching looks like as it is being serged. We look in front of the needle so much we forget to check the results as they come out the back of the serger. A thread that is snagged or wrapped around something can cause some funny looking stitches. You can often repair a problem with minimal effort if you catch it soon enough.

Don't serge over pins. This will damage your knife blades. Learn to "finger pin" as you serge and use as few pins as possible. Try to use pins with large heads in a contrasting color to the fabric. Place pins at a 90° angle several inches from the edge of the fabric so they are out of the way as you serge by them.

Make sure the thread is feeding off the spools properly. If the thread is caught or twisted, you will have skipped or irregular stitches, broken thread, or tension problems.

Check the position of the blade before serging. Make sure the blade is either fully engaged in position to cut or is totally disengaged. Turn the blade or knob until it fully clicks in or out of place.

Don't pull the fabric as you serge. Let the feed dogs pull the fabric through the serger. All you need do is guide the fabric and let the serger do the work. You can bend the needles by pulling the fabric.

Cleaning

Oil your machine regularly with good sewing machine oil. Use *only* sewing machine oil. All sergers need oiling. Check your manual for specifics on where to put the oil. You should oil most sergers about every eight to ten hours of use. If it has been sitting unused for a while, oil it before using.

Clean the lint and fabric out of your machine often. Use ozone-safe canned air and a small brush. Makeup brushes are great for cleaning lint from sergers. You can also buy a set of small attachments for the vacuum cleaner designed for use with machines, computers, and other equipment. These attachments can be found in vacuum and sewing stores or through mail order.

Have your serger serviced regularly. You can't get all the lint out of your serger with canned air or with the vacuum cleaner. It builds up over time inside the machine. A qualified repair person will take the cover off to clean and oil the places you can't reach. This will keep your serger running smoothly for many years.

Troubleshooting

I highly recommend that you get a copy of *The Ultimate Serger Answer Guide* (see the Bibliography) to answer your troubleshooting questions and other issues that can't be adequately covered in this section. Following are some of the basic issues you may run into when using decorative threads.

Improper Tension. If you can't get the tensions to adjust properly, check to make sure the thread is properly seated between the tension disks. If you can see the thread, it isn't as far between the disks as it should be. Reduce the tension all the way, then reset it so the thread will fall in place. You can also grip the thread at either side of the dial by hand and pull it in place between the disks inside the dials.

Skipped Stitches. Make sure the machine is threaded properly and in the correct order. Make sure all the threads are feeding evenly. Change the needles. Check that you're using the right kind of needle. Loosen the tension on the thread that is skipping.

Thread or Fabric Jam. Jamming occurs when thread builds up on the stitch finger and keeps the fabric from feeding through under the foot. This can happen when:

❶ serging without putting the presser foot down
❷ using heavy decorative thread
❸ serging a tightly rolled edge
❹ using a short stitch length
❺ the knife is disengaged and fabric gets caught in the loopers
❻ all of the above
❼ Who knows? Maybe gremlins.

Don't try to sew it out. Stop serging. The thread will only keep building up on the stitch finger. Gently pull the chain to see if you can remove the jam. You may need to reduce all the tensions to zero so the thread will slip off the stitch finger. If

you can't gently tug the thread off without force, take a small pair of sharp pointed scissors and cut the threads loose. You may need to remove the foot to have better access to the stitch finger area. If the needles are caught in the fabric, loosen the needle screws, cut the thread, and pull the needles out of the fabric by hand or with tweezers. Put in new needles when the jam is cleared.

This problem can often be avoided by clearing the stitch finger before you start to serge. Gently pull the chain of thread off the stitch finger when starting to serge until a few stitches have been taken into the fabric. The weight of the fabric will then push the thread through on its own.

Jamming can also occur when serging with the blade disengaged. If the fabric goes too far over the edge of the plate, it will get tangled up with the loopers. Always guide the fabric exactly along the edge of the needle plate when the blade is disengaged.

Use a blind hem foot to guide the edge of the fabric to serge without cutting. Be sure to check your manual for the correct needle position to use with the blind hem foot. Many sergers have blind hem feet that will only let you use the right needle position, which gives you a much narrower stitch width. Some sergers have fabric guides that screw into the front of the serger that keep the fabric from being cut.

Creative Serging & Sewing Techniques

CHAPTER 4

Serger Techniques

On a sewing machine, you push a button or turn a knob to select a stitch. Many sewing machines also require that you adjust the stitch length, stitch width, and tension before the selected stitch is properly set. On a serger, you have to turn the tension dials to change from one type of stitch to another. This also requires that you adjust the stitch length and width to achieve the desired stitch setting. Don't be afraid to turn the tension dials!

This chapter describes the serger techniques used for the garments featured in this book. You won't find the exact tension settings to use on your serger because they vary too much from brand to brand. Your serger manual will give you recommended settings to use for your model. Experiment with these techniques to get the right setting. The more familiar you are with your serger, the more versatile it will be. This is just a starting point.

The only time I use all four (or five) threads is for construction seams that hold the garment together. You can also construct with two or three threads when using decorative thread for the stitching to show on the right side. All the decorative techniques used for projects in this book are done using either two- or three-thread techniques. Final garment construction is done with a balanced four-thread stitch.

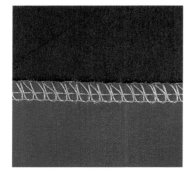

Top side of a balanced four-thread construction stitch.

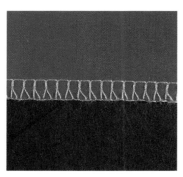

Bottom side of a balanced four-thread construction stitch.

Balanced Stitch Vs. Unbalanced Stitch

A balanced stitch means the looper threads interlock at the cut edge of the fabric and the needle stitch shows as a small dot on the back of the fabric. An unbalanced stitch means the looper threads don't interlock at the edge of the fabric (as in a rolled edge), or when the needle thread tension is loosened to allow the seam to open up (as in a flatlock).

Stitches Used for Garment Embellishments
Balanced Four-Thread Construction Stitch

The construction stitch is a balanced four-thread stitch primarily used to hold a seam together. Adjust the tensions so the looper threads meet exactly at the cut edge of the fabric. Determine the width by the weight of the fabric. Use a narrow width for lightweight fabrics, a medium width for medium weight fabrics, and a wide width for heavy fabrics. An average construction stitch length of 2½ to 3 is best for most fabrics. If the stitch length is too short, it can perforate the fabric at the seamline, causing the fibers to weaken. If the stitch length is too long, there will be gaps between the stitches from the right side.

Balanced Three-Thread Decorative Stitch

Only one needle is used for this stitch in your choice of left or right needle position. The needle position determines the stitch width. This stitch can be used as a decorative construction stitch or as a decorative edge finish, depending on the type of thread. Adjust the tensions so the looper threads meet exactly at the cut edge of the fabric.

Two-Thread Chain Stitch

This stitch is available on five-thread sergers. Only two threads are used for a chain stitch. The blade and upper looper are disengaged and a flatbed extension table is snapped in place to allow stitching anywhere on the fabric without cutting. When a decorative thread is used in the chain stitch looper, you will have many options for embellishments. This stitch looks great on plain or scrunched fabric. Serge with the right side of the fabric toward the feed dogs.

Top side of a balanced three-thread decorative stitch.

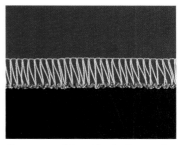

Bottom side of a balanced three-thread decorative stitch.

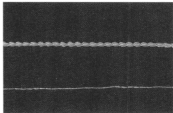

Both sides of a two-thread chain stitch.

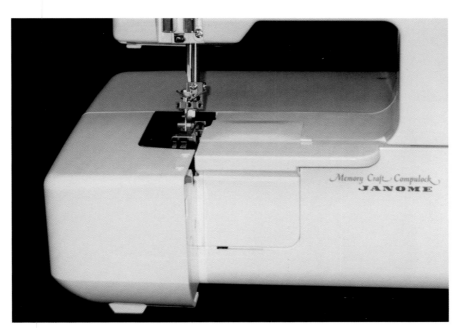

Serger set up for chain stitch using the flatbed extension table.

TIP

Slow down when doing any kind of decorative serging! You will have more control of the fabric and the stitch quality will be more consistent.

Flatlock Stitch

A flatlock stitch is made with either two or three threads. The flatlock stitch opens up to make a flat seam with the raw edges enclosed inside. It is a stitch that is both decorative and functional and you will find many places to use it.

Let the thread loops hang about 1/8" off the edge of thick fabric when serging so the stitches will flatten out more. A blind hem foot will guide the fabric away from the blade so you don't have to worry about accidentally cutting the fabric. Some blind hem feet are designed to use the right needle position only, which makes a narrower stitch width. In this case, it's better not to use the blind hem foot. Instead, guide the fabric yourself so you can use the left needle position and get the widest stitch possible. Follow the blind hem foot instructions for your serger.

Use any stitch length or width that you like as long as it's suitable for the fabric you are using. Changing the stitch length and width will produce different looks. Use the left needle for a wide stitch, the right needle for a narrow stitch. Experiment with combining different types of decorative threads and/or different color combinations for creating your own color coordinated trims.

For a three-thread flatlock stitch, loosen the needle tension almost or all the way to the lowest setting. This allows the seam to be opened flat. Set the upper looper at a balanced normal setting. Tighten the lower looper tension almost all the way so the looper thread is almost straight along the edge of the fabric. Make sure the lower looper is not too tight or the fabric will draw up as you serge The stitches will begin to unravel at the ends if the thread is cut too short.

For a two-thread flatlock stitch, engage the upper looper converter. Refer to your serger manual to convert to two-thread serging. The two-thread flatlock stitch uses the lower looper and either needle position. The needle tension is loosened enough to reach the cut edge of the fabric where it should interlock with the lower looper thread.

TIP

A flatlock stitch works well on most types of fabric. If the fabric is not sturdy enough to hold the stitch without raveling apart, fuse iron-on knit interfacing to the wrong side of the fabric.

Ladders and Loops

When this stitch is opened up, the upper looper thread forms the loops and the loosened needle thread forms the ladders. You can use either side of this stitch for decorative serging.

Serge the fabric right-sides-together if you want the ladders to show on the right side. Put decorative thread in the needle for either a two- or three-thread flatlock.

Serge the fabric wrong-sides-together if you want the loops to show on the right side. Put decorative thread in the upper looper for a three-thread flatlock and in the lower looper for a two-thread flatlock.

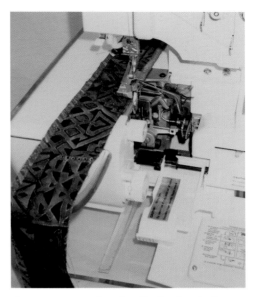

Serger set up for the flatlock stitch.

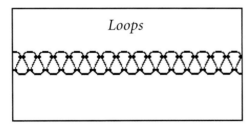

Serge fabric wrong sides together.

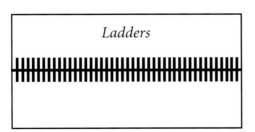

Serge fabric right sides together.

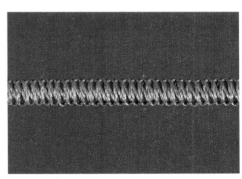

Loop side.

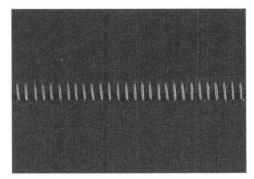

Ladder side.

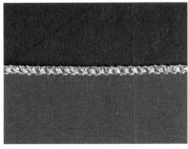

Rolled edge stitch with rayon thread.

Serger set up for the rolled edge stitch.

Top side of rolled edge stitch with heavy decorative thread.

Bottom side of rolled edge stitch with heavy decorative thread.

Rolled Edge Stitch

The terms "rolled edge" and "rolled hem" refer to the same stitch. I use the term rolled edge throughout the instructions to maintain consistency and to keep from implying that the technique is being used to make a hem.

Refer to your manual for specific instructions on setting up your serger to make a rolled edge. Some models have a built-in lever that disengages the larger stitch finger by sliding it toward the front of the serger, leaving the rolled edge stitch finger in place. Others require that you completely remove the larger stitch finger or change the needle plate and/or presser foot. Rolled edge accessories are usually marked with an R.

Set the stitch length to 1 for a filled-in satin stitch look. Set the length to a higher number for a more open look. By combining these adjustments with the use of the narrow stitch finger, the edge of the fabric will fold over inside the stitches and give you a more durable finished edge.

If the stitched fabric puckers lengthwise, either the needle tension or the lower looper tension may be too tight. A too-short stitch length can also cause puckers. Make adjustments until the fabric lies flat after stitching.

The trick to making a great rolled edge is in the tension settings you use.

A three-thread rolled edge is done with one needle (usually the right needle) and both loopers. The upper looper tension may need to be loosened a little so the thread can wrap around the edge of the fabric and completely cover the underside. The lower looper tension should be tightened until it looks like a straight line of thread just next to the needle thread on the bottom. You may also have to tighten the needle tension a little so it's not pulled loose by the tightened thread of the lower looper.

A two-thread rolled edge is done using the lower looper and one needle. Adjust the lower looper tension so the thread can wrap around the edge of the fabric and completely cover the both sides of the fabric. You may also have to tighten the needle tension a little so it doesn't look loose on the wrong side of the fabric.

Serger Chain Braid

There are many ways to make custom braid and trim on a serger. The look of the braid is mainly determined by the stitch settings used. To stabilize the stitches of wide three-thread serger chain braid, you can serge over ribbon, yarn, water soluble stabilizer, Seams Great, or cording. Refer to the book *Deco Serging* by April Dunn for a variety of wide trims and braids that can be made on the serger.

The garments in this book have been made with narrow two- and three-thread serger chain braid. You can make great serger chain braid when you blend colors and mix types of thread. All types of thread can be used and combined to make decorative serger chain braids.

Make more braid than you think you'll need for the embellishments. It's easy to get carried away once you get started, but leftovers can always be used in other projects.

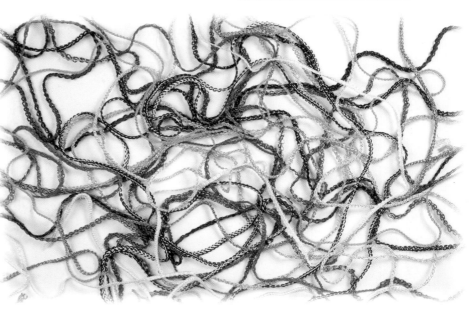

Serger chain braid made with various types of decorative thread.

Serger Setup

Three-Thread Rolled Edge. To make the serger chain braid, refer to your manual and adjust the serger for a three-thread rolled edge. Thread both loopers with heavier decorative threads and use a thinner thread for the needle. Start with a stitch length of 2 and set both looper tensions a bit lower than the normal settings. Set the needle tension at normal. Play with the tensions and stitch length as you serge a couple of yards until you like the way the chain looks.

Two-Thread Chain Stitch Braid. This braid is narrower and looks quite different from three-thread braid. This type of braid can be couched on the fabric and is also great for making tassels and fringe.

Two-Thread Chain Stitch. Refer to your manual to adjust the serger for a two-thread chain stitch. Put a thick decorative thread in the chain stitch looper and a thinner decorative thread in the needle. You may have to start stitching on a small piece of fabric to get the chain started.

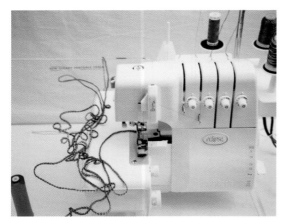

Keep the chain taut as you make serger chain braid.

Making Serger Chain Braid

Keep the serger going at a moderate, steady speed (not too slow, not too fast). Gently but steadily pull the chain as it comes out from under the foot. You don't want the thread to build up on the stitch finger so you have to help it by putting tension on the chain as it feeds out the back of the serger. Just keep the chain moving out from under the foot. Don't pull very hard or you might bend the needle backward and possibly break it. You will develop a rhythm with a little practice.

Chain Serging

Chain serging helps minimize stretching and distortion when joining many pieces together. It also saves a lot of time. It's important not to cut the chain of strips off the serger. Cut them off only when they are to be joined to another section. This keeps everything in order so the strips can be serged together in the proper sequence.

1 To chain the strips, lay the fabric out in the correct serging order. Pick up the first piece of fabric to the left in your left hand. Pick up the piece next to it on the right in your right hand. Place the right piece on top of the left piece. This puts the fabric in the correct position for serging. Place them under the foot and serge the seam. Follow this order each time you pick up the fabric and your seams will always be on the correct side and won't get out of order.

2 Serge the strips together, doing only two at a time. Don't cut them from the serger. This will keep the strips in order.

3 When all the strips are serged in pairs, don't cut the thread. Find the first set of strips at the beginning of the chain. Begin with that pair of strips and serge the pairs together two at a time. Only cut the strips off the end as you join them to another set. Always start serging from the same end so the direction of the stitching is consistent.

4 Continue serging the sections together two at a time until all are joined together.

Chain the strips in order and keep them attached to the serger until needed.

TIP

To speed up the process of rethreading, you can cut the old thread, tie on the new thread, reduce the tensions, and pull it through the guides.

Final Vest Construction on the Serger

Follow these instructions to construct a vest entirely on the serger.

Serger Setup: Balanced Four-Thread Construction Stitch

Set up your serger for a balanced four-thread construction stitch with size 11 universal needles. Use polyester thread in the needles and loopers. Use a wide stitch width and a stitch length of 2½. Test your stitch settings and adjust by serging four layers of fabric.

Serging: Final Construction

❶ Serge the shoulder seams of the lining front and back, right-sides-together. Serge the shoulder seams of the outer vest front and back, right-sides-together.

❷ Lay the two vests on top of each other, right-sides-together. Serge around the front hems, neckline, front edges, armscyes, and back hem. Don't serge the side seams yet. You will turn the vest right-side-out through the side seam.

❸ Press the stitching flat from the wrong side before turning. Turn the vest right-side-out through one of the back side seams. Press again from the right side.

❹ Line up the cut edges of the front and back side seams. Reach through the inside of the vest back, from one side seam all the way through to the opposite side seam. Grasp the cut

TIP

For wrapped corners at the points and/or corners of the vest, fold over the serged seam exactly on the needle thread line at the corner and serge over it as you start the next seam. This helps you turn the points to the outside more easily.

Vest Construction on Serger

Serge in the direction of the arrows

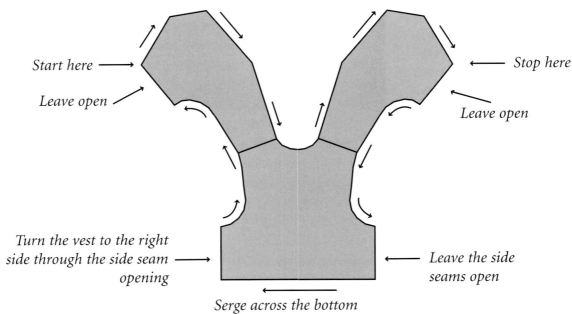

Start here →   Leave open   Turn the vest to the right side through the side seam opening →   Serge across the bottom ←   Stop here   Leave open   Leave the side seams open

55

edges of the front and back side seams, lining up the edges. Bring all the layers back through the side seam openings and line up the crossing seamlines at the underarm and bottom hem line, forming a circle. When you pull the side seams through the remaining side seam, it will become a circle within a circle. Start on the lining side and serge around the circle, completely closing up one side seam. Let the seam go back in place inside the vest.

⑤ Line up the cut edges of the remaining front and back side seams, matching the seamlines at the underarm and the bottom hem line. Start serging on the lining fabric about 2" before the seams cross at the bottom hem. Serge a few inches, then stop with the needle down and realign the edges. The seam will be closing up as you serge it. Serge the side seam together on the remaining side as far as you can. Be sure to watch for the layer of fabric that will be underneath and on top of the two layers you are serging together. Slipstitch the opening closed by hand. Topstitch around the vest with your sewing machine if desired.

Securing Seams

Don't cut the thread off at the edge of the fabric - always leave a 4" to 6" chain of thread on both the serger and fabric. This will allow enough thread at each end of the fabric so that any method can be used to secure the seams.

If you are going to cross one seam with another seam, the new stitching will lock off the thread.

Tie Off. Skinny out the chain of thread by gripping it close to the foot and pulling along the length of it with your fingernails to stretch it out. Make a loose overhand knot and pull it down toward the edge of the fabric. Insert a straight pin through the larger loop of the knot and through the edge of the fabric right where the stitching ends. Push the pin halfway through the fabric. Place your thumb and forefinger underneath the pin to support both sides of it. Pull the end of the thread chain with the other hand to tighten the knot to the edge of the fabric. Use seam sealant on the knot and cut off the excess thread when dry.

Lock Stitch at Both Ends of the Seam. Make one or two stitches in the fabric and stop. Raise the presser foot and hold the fabric in place while you skinny out the chain of thread. Bring the thread under and to the front of the foot. Let the excess thread chain hang in front of the knife to be cut off. Continue serging to the end of the seam. Stop before serging off the edge of the fabric. Turn the flywheel by hand and make

Beginning lock stitch.

one or two stitches off the end of the fabric. Raise the presser foot and gently tug the fabric to slip the thread off the stitch finger. Flip the fabric over, turn it around, and place it back under the foot. Lower the presser foot and serge over the previous stitching for about an inch before serging off the edge. Be careful to angle the fabric away from the blade so you don't cut into the previous stitching.

Tuck the Thread Chain Inside the Stitches. Place the chain through the eye of a large eye or double eye needle. Run the needle through the back side of the stitching for about an inch.

Ending lock stitch.

Pull the needle tight and cut the chain close to the needle exit, allowing the cut end of the thread to slip inside the serger stitches. Use a dot of seam sealant to keep the threads from fraying.

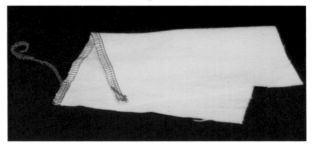

Fabric lock stitched at both ends.

Removing Balanced Stitches

Pull the Needle Threads. Trim the chain at one end of the seam to the edge of the fabric. From the other end, work the needle threads out of the chain and pull them as if you were gathering the fabric (the needle threads are the shortest threads in the chain). Continue to pull the threads completely out of the seam. The looper threads will come right off when the needle thread has been removed. If you have a long seam to remove, remove the needle thread in shorter sections. This method won't work as well if the stitch length is very close together or if the fabric creates resistance to the thread being pulled through it.

Clip the Needle Threads. If you can't get the needle threads to pull out of the seam, here's an alternative. Clip the needle threads every few stitches with a seam ripper or a small pair of pointed scissors. Don't cut through the looper threads. After clipping the needle threads, gently pull both looper threads to remove the stitches, then separate the layers of fabric to loosen any remaining needle threads, making stitch removal quite simple.

Removing Flatlock Stitches. It's very easy to remove a three-thread flatlock stitch. Separate the chain and find the lower looper thread. It will be running straight along the edge of the fabric, holding the needle and upper looper threads together. Pull the lower looper thread out of the stitching and the other threads will release.

A two-thread flatlock stitch isn't quite as easy to remove. Cut through the needle thread with a small pair of pointed scissors. Pull the lower looper thread off the fabric. Remove any excess threads with tape.

Removing Rolled Edge Stitches. This stitch takes a little more effort to remove than the others, especially when a short stitch length has been used. Use a seam ripper or razor cutter to carefully cut the needle thread. Pull away the looper thread in a continuous piece. If you can afford to lose the width of the stitch from your fabric, it's easier and quicker to use a rotary cutter and ruler to cut away the entire seam and start fresh with a new rolled edge.

Fabric Manipulation

Scrunched Fabric

My first exposure to this fabric manipulation technique was from the book *Design & Sew it Yourself - A Workbook for Creative Clothing* written by Lois and Diane Ericson in 1983. They referred to it as "wrinkled and stitched fabric." This technique was revised for the '90s in the book *Creating Texture with Textiles* by Linda McGehee, who calls it "crinkled fabric." It has also been called "random wrinkles," "planned wrinkles," and "scrunched fabric." I like "scrunched fabric" best to describe this technique. No matter what term is used, it all refers to the same basic technique. There are some variations in the steps taken by different designers to achieve the same effects. As is true in most everything we do, there's more than one way to accomplish the same result. Feel free to play and experiment with the techniques of different designers and use the method you feel most comfortable with.

See the Bibliography for further information on this type of fabric manipulation.

This is one of my absolute favorite fabric manipulations. I love to take scrunched fabric and cover it with serger chain braid, fancy threads, yarns of all types, and decorative stitches from the sewing machine. The finished fabric can be used as yoke overlays, strips in patchwork, appliquÈs, and for entire garment sections.

How Much Fabric to Scrunch

❶ Measure the length and width of the pattern to determine the size of the finished fabric needed. Add three inches in both directions to the total. The length of the fabric is not affected by scrunching it.

❷ The fabric to be scrunched should be at least 1½ times wider than the width needed for the finished piece. The width is with the crossgrain, from selvage to selvage. It's better to have too much than not enough.

Scrunching the Fabric

1 Start with wet or damp fabric. Run it through the rinse and spin cycle of the washing machine to wet it and remove the excess water. You can also wet it with a spray bottle or in the sink but be sure to wring out as much water as you can before scrunching. It takes longer to dry if the fabric is too wet.

2 Lay the wet fabric out flat on a table or flat surface. Begin at one selvage edge and accordion fold the fabric into small pleats until you reach the other selvage. Hold the pleats in your hands as you go. Don't let go or the pleats will fall out and you'll have to start over.

3 Grip the pleated fabric at each end and twist it until it folds back up on itself into a tight ball. You may need a friend to hold one end of the fabric while you do this. Place rubber bands around the twisted fabric to hold it in place.

4 Let the fabric dry. I usually let it air dry but that takes a couple of days so I scrunch my fabric a few days before I plan to work with it. You can also put it in a clothes dryer with a towel to cushion it. This is a much quicker way, but it still takes several hours for the fabric to dry.

Scrunch the fabric from selvage to selvage.

Experiment with different ways to twist the fabric. You can't mess it up. If you don't like the results, wet the fabric and twist it again. Not all fabrics will wrinkle the same. Thin fabrics will wrinkle a lot more than thick ones. Fiber content also affects the amount of wrinkling - fabrics made from natural fibers wrinkle the best.

We have all bought fabrics that looked good on the bolt but became a wrinkled mess after washing. Go through your fabric stash and scrunch up all those wrinkled pieces. Leave them twisted until needed.

Twist the fabric into a ball.

TIP

I usually use the entire width of the fabric. I don't think you can ever have too much. I have scrunched myself into a corner a few times and had to really get creative to figure out how to make do with less than what was needed. Use a little more fabric than you think is needed so you don't find yourself standing in the corner too.

TIP

Cut the fabric to the length needed for scrunching before prewashing it. Twist it up before placing it in the dryer.

Fusing Interfacing to the Scrunched Fabric

Weaving board

Stretch out the scrunched fabric to the size of the interfacing. Place the wrong side of the fabric to the fusible side of the interfacing. Pin the fabric in place around the edges. Fuse starting from the center.

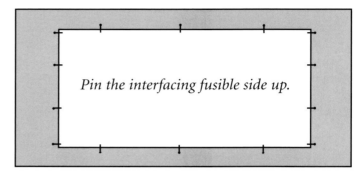

Pin the interfacing fusible side up.

Portable iron and pinning surface

The size of the interfacing determines the density of the wrinkles. I start with a piece of scrunched fabric that starts out approximately 42" to 45" wide and fuse it to a piece of interfacing the length of the fabric and 30" wide. The 30" width is a sufficient size to cut most embellishments.

Most knit interfacing is 20" wide but it also comes 60" wide. If using the larger width, you won't have to piece it to get the correct size. When piecing sections of interfacing together, overlap the edges and fuse. Use a Teflon pressing sheet to keep the interfacing from sticking to your ironing equipment.

❶ Pin the interfacing fusible-side-up to the weaving/ironing board at each corner and along the sides.

❷ Open the scrunched fabric, wrong side of the fabric to the fusible side of the interfacing. Stretch it out to fit the size of the interfacing. Pin the four corners of the fabric to the interfacing and distribute the wrinkles evenly. Finish pinning the fabric around the outer edges. Use quite a few pins to hold the scrunched fabric in place for pressing. Place the pins at an angle away from the center of the fabric so it will be easier to press all the way to the edges.

❸ Start pressing from the middle of the fabric and continue fusing out to the edges. Use a press cloth to protect the fabric. Don't slide the iron over the fabric - set it straight down on the fabric and hold it in place while fusing, then pick it straight up. Move the iron to another place on the fabric and repeat until everything is well fused. Turn the fabric over and finish pressing from the interfacing side.

The scrunched fabric is now ready to embellish or use as is.

Right side of scrunched fabric.

Wrong side of scrunched fabric.

Right side of scrunched fabric couched with serger chain braid.

Wrong side of scrunched fabric couched with serger chain braid.

Sewing Machine Techniques

Stitching Serger Chain Braid to Fabric

Serger chain braid can be stitched on fabric that is flat (as is), pieced, or scrunched. Always use a stabilizer under the fabric to keep the stitching from drawing it up. For scrunched fabric, the knit interfacing ironed on the back eliminates the need for additional stabilizer.

Sewing Machine Setup: Zigzag Stitch

❶ Set the sewing machine for a medium width zigzag stitch.

❷ Use a braid, cording, or couching foot to guide the braid as it is stitched in place. Stitch some braid on a piece of practice fabric to determine the length, width, and tension setting for the look you want. I usually set a stitch length of 2 and a width between 2 and 3.

❸ Reduce the upper tension 1 to 2 numbers from the normal setting so the bobbin thread doesn't show on the right side.

❹ Start on one edge of the fabric and meander to the other side while stitching over the braid.

❺ Change the colors of braid and top thread several times.

❻ Using a press cloth, press the stitched fabric from the wrong side.

I usually keep stitching until it looks right to me. Sometimes I stitch the braid on quite heavily and other times I use less. It depends on the colors and types of thread I'm using. I usually lighten up when using metallic threads because a little of that can go a long way. Sometimes the fabric is so pretty in its unembellished state that I don't want to cover it very heavily with serger chain braid. Each garment tells me what to do as I'm making it. There is no wrong way to do this. This is a technique that releases you from having to follow any rules. Keep stitching until it looks good to you and have fun!

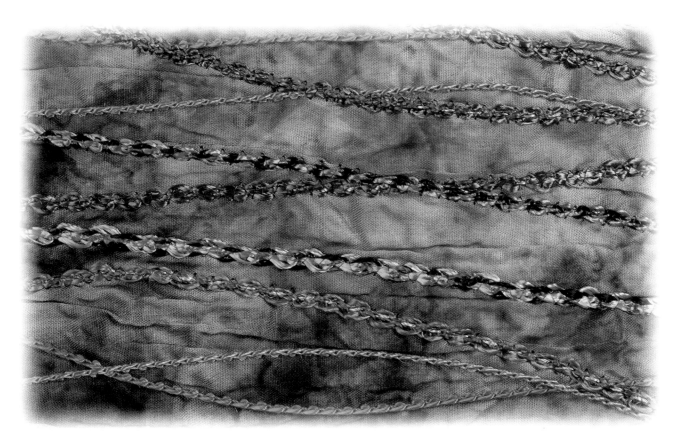

Combination of two-thread chain stitch with decorative thread in the looper and serger braid stitched with a sewing machine on scrunched fabric.

CHAPTER 5

Threads for the Creative Serger

How & Where to Use Decorative Threads

The garments in this book have been embellished with many different types of decorative thread. This chapter covers many types of thread that can be used in a serger and gives suggestions for how to use them. At the end of the chapter are some basic guidelines to follow when using decorative thread. There are many serger techniques that give you much room for creativity. Most decorative serging is a matter of personal preference (in other words, anything goes!).

You can serge decorative thread directly on the fabric. Make your own decorative piping, ribbon, and trims, or make different kinds of serger braid and apply it by using a zigzag stitch or a twin needle and stitching over it with a conventional sewing machine. You can mix and match thread types and colors to create your own custom embellishments. Not all sergers use heavy thread in both loopers, so experiment and see what works best in your serger.

If using decorative thread on the serger for the first time, start with woolly nylon and 30 to 40 weight rayon thread. These are the easiest threads to work with. As you get more comfortable, experiment with other types of thread available for serger use. Soon you will be serging with anything you can get through the eye of the loopers.

Photocopy or scan the "Stitch Setting Chart" on page 71. The chart is designed to be placed in a notebook with a sample attached. Keep the best sample of each stitch. Write on the chart the tension settings and any special instructions that apply to your serger.

Be patient and take time to experiment as you learn these techniques. Serging with decorative thread is a lot of fun and reduces stress and helps you to feel good about creating something. You can create one-of-a-kind works of art to wear, sell, or give as gifts. Soon people will stop you to get a closer look at what you are wearing!

Threads for Creative Serging

What types of thread can be used for creative serging? Following are some of the many types of thread you can use in your serger. Because there are so many, this is not a full description of all brands of thread.

Cotton, Polyester, and Blends (American & Efrid, Mettler).

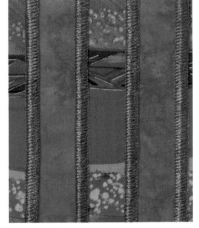

Flatlock stitch with two strands of 30 wt. rayon thread in the upper looper.

Flatlock stitch with 30 wt. rayon thread in the needle.

Regular size spools of thread can be used on a serger. Use the spool caps provided with your machine so the thread feeds off smoothly. Large cones of thread designed for serger use are a lot more economical than small spools. Use cotton thread for quilt piecing, extra fine cotton thread for heirloom serging, polyester thread for seams or in the needles when using other types of thread in the loopers. Polyester thread is usually used in the needle when using decorative thread in the loopers. Use the regular thread spindles.

Silk, Rayon, and Acrylic Machine Embroidery Thread (Sulky, Janome, Madeira, YLI, American & Efird, Coats Mez Alcazar). Silk and rayon threads have a beautiful finish. Use these anywhere the stitching will show or with like fabrics. Machine embroidery thread is lightweight and has a duller finish but comes in many beautiful colors. Use Sulky rayon thread in the upper looper to make a beautiful rolled edge. Sulky makes 30 and 40 weight rayon thread. Make serger appliqués, hem curtains, flatlock stitches, etc. A ThreadPRO or horizontal spool pin will prevent the thread from twisting and/or breaking as it feeds off the spool. Use a thread palette to blend up to five colors of thread.

Metallic (Sulky, Madeira, American & Efird, YLI). Metallic thread comes in a wide range of colors. You can blend metallic thread with other decorative thread to add a little sparkle to your garment or use it by itself for a lot of sparkle. If the metallic thread frays or breaks in the lower looper, use it in the upper looper only and put a different type of thread in the lower looper. A ThreadPRO or horizontal spool pin will prevent the thread from twisting and/or breaking as it feeds off the spool. Another trick to reduce breakage is to use Sulky invisible thread together with the metallic in the same looper.

Sliver (Sulky) **and Tinsel Thread** (Stream Lamé). Sliver is a very narrow flat strip of polyester film covered with a metallic coating. It can be used alone or blended with other thread in the loopers. Don't use it anywhere next to the skin because it's too scratchy. Use a horizontal spool pin so the thread won't twist and/or break as it feeds off the spool. If this thread continues to break, thread a spool of Sulky invisible thread through the same tension disk. Adjust the tension to allow for the two threads. A ThreadPRO or horizontal spool pin will prevent the thread from twisting and/or breaking as it feeds off the spool.

Texturized Nylon (Woolly Nylon, Mettler, YLI). This fuzzy looking thread works great on knits, spandex, rolled edges,

home decorating projects, crafts, and a great deal more. When used in the needles, it stretches with the seams in stretch fabric. It spreads out to fill in the space between stitches in a rolled hem to give it a satiny, durable finish. It's perfect for hemming clothing, curtains, ruffles, and home decorator items, but remember not to iron it with a hot iron or it will melt. Metallic Woolly Nylon comes in many colors and has a metallic thread twisted through it. Woolly Nylon Extra is three times as thick and gives a lot more coverage than regular Woolly. Use the regular thread spindles.

Sulky Invisible Thread. This polyester monofilament thread is a really fine (.004) invisible thread that is both soft and strong. It comes in clear and smoke colors to blend with any fabric. It is my personal favorite to use as a top thread when couching serger braid on with the sewing machine. The polyester withstands more heat than nylon invisible thread. I press a lot when I sew and I don't want to worry about melting the thread off my project. You can also run it through the same tension disk with a spool of Sulky Sliver if you have any problems with the Sliver breaking.

Clear Nylon Filament. This monofilament invisible thread can be used in weights from 40 lb. test fishing line to size 80. Serge over the heavier weights, enclosing it in the stitching, or use the lighter weights in the serger for invisible stitching. Serge over fishing line with a rolled edge to give more flounce to the edge of a ruffle. Invisible thread can be used in the needles and loopers and blends with any color. Use thread nets to keep it from slipping off the spool as it feeds. Use it in the needle and lower looper with a decorative thread in the upper looper. The decorative thread will appear to be floating on top of the fabric. You can serge over beads, sequins, and ribbons with clear thread in the needle and loopers. Because nylon thread is a little scratchy, don't use it in seams that will rub against the skin.

Decor 6 (Madeira) **and Designer 6** (YLI). Decor 6 is a thick, loosely twisted rayon thread with beautiful shine that looks good as a decorative edge on anything! Use it in one or both loopers. Use a rayon, polyester, or invisible thread in the needle. A ThreadPRO or horizontal spool pin will prevent the thread from twisting and/or breaking as it feeds off the spool.

#7 Floss (Robison-Anton). This is a thick, lightly twisted rayon thread. It is slightly smaller than the size 6 thread and comes on a one-pound cone that can be wound onto smaller spools using the E-Z Winder.

Decor 12 (Madeira). Decor 12 is a lightly twisted rayon thread thinner than size 6 and 7. It has a beautiful shine and looks good as a decorative edge. Use it in one or both loopers with a rayon, polyester, or invisible thread in the needle. Use a ThreadPRO or a horizontal spool pin so the thread won't twist and/or break as it feeds off the spool.

Candlelight (YLI). This soft, thick metallic thread is very compatible with Designer 6, pearl cotton, and pearl rayon when used in the loopers. Use it anywhere you want the glitter of metallics.

Pearl Cotton (Mettler) **and Pearl Crown Rayon** (YLI). These threads are very soft and the rayon has a beautiful luster. Use in one or both loopers with polyester thread in the needle. These are great for edging baby items, heavy fabrics, and for flatlock stitching on crafts and garments.

Crochet Thread. There are many different weights of cotton and acrylic crochet thread that can be used on a serger. If it is not too thick or stiff, it can be used in both loopers. Be sure to preshrink cotton crochet thread before you use it. Submerge the entire ball of thread in hot water and leave it until the water cools. Remove the ball from the water and put it in a colander to drain. It may take a few days to dry completely. If you need it really fast, place the wet ball in a pillowcase and tie it off as close to the ball of thread as you can. Throw it in the dryer with a couple of lightweight items. Be warned - this "quickie" method can sometimes cause the thread to come unwound and tangle up inside the pillowcase.

Use crochet thread in combination with invisible thread if you want the loops to look like they are floating on the fabric. This looks good on baby items and heavy fabrics like denim and terry cloth. Use it as cording to serge over for gathering.

Punch Needle Embroidery Thread. There are several brands of punch needle embroidery thread and many types of textures available in each brand, from smooth cotton to fuzzy yarn. This type of thread can be found in many craft stores wound on cardboard tubes and can be put right on the regular thread spindle.

Silk or Polyester Ribbon. Very soft ribbon can be used in the upper looper. It can be from 1/16″ to 1/8″ wide, but 1/8″ ribbon must be very soft to feed evenly through the looper. Ribbon works well on baby items, sweater knits, and children's wear. You can also serge over the ribbon with a long stitch length if it's too wide to use in the loopers. Use a ThreadPRO or a horizontal spool pin so the thread won't twist and/or break as it feeds off the spool.

Ribbon Floss. Ribbon floss is available in many colors in rayon or metallic fiber. It can be used in the upper looper alone for a single-sided edging or in both loopers for a double-sided edging on capes, jackets, place mats, etc. This thread is great to use for making serger chain braid. There isn't much yardage on a spool, 40 yards of rayon and 30 yards of metallic, so plan accordingly. Use a ThreadPRO or a horizontal spool pin so the thread won't twist as it feeds off the spool.

Topstitching, Buttonhole Twist, Jeans Stitch, and Quilting Thread (American & Efird, Mettler, YLI). These are tightly twisted, thick, cord-like threads. They are very durable and can be used in the needles and loopers when a strong seam is needed. Use a topstitching needle so there will be room for the thread to pass through the eye. Use this type of thread in the upper looper only for a rolled edge, balanced three-thread decorative stitch, and flatlock on medium to heavyweight fabrics.

Yarn and Luny. Thin smooth yarns can be used if they are small and smooth enough to go through the eye of the loopers. You will have to wind these on a spool to use on the serger. Yarn can be used in the loopers for seams on sweater knits and wool fabrics. Use it for edging baby items and knitted clothing. Luny is a very thin, yarn-like thread wound on a cardboard tube ready to be used on the serger. It has a fine, fuzzy texture. Use it in the loopers as you would yarn.

Guidelines for Using Decorative Threads In Your Serger

• Serge slowly and maintain a steady speed. Serging too fast can cause dropped or uneven stitches and sudden starting and stopping can affect the stitch quality. Sometimes it is very important to have control over the stitching and you will need to turn the flywheel by hand. Just because a serger can stitch fast doesn't mean you have to serge at top speed. The speedometer in my car goes up to 80 mph, but I don't go that fast everywhere I drive.

• Before serging on a project, always serge a test sample to adjust the settings using the same fabric and number of layers you will be using in the project.

• When using heavy threads, start with a wide stitch width and adjust it to get the desired look. Use the widest stitch width on medium to heavyweight fabrics and a narrow width on lightweight fabrics.

• Start with a longer stitch length and shorten it to get the desired look. Large thread fills up more space than small thread and requires a longer stitch length.

• Large threads require looser than normal tension settings (lower numbers) and conversely, small threads require tighter than normal tension settings (higher numbers).

• On some sergers you may have to totally bypass the tension dial when using heavy thread in the loopers or in the needle position to get a nice flatlock stitch. Thread through all the other thread guides but don't put the thread in the tension dial. If you have drop-in tension dials, put tape over the top groove of the serger (where the tension dial is) so the thread will ride on top of the tape instead of in the dial.

• Always lift up the presser foot and place fabric under it before serging. This helps maintain uniform stitching and keeps the fabric layers from shifting.

• Use a new needle for each decorative project to insure the best stitch quality. This helps prevent skipped stitches in the middle of a project.

• Use thread nets when serging with slippery rayon, acrylic, or metallic threads that slide down on the spool. Using a net adds extra tension to the thread. Be aware of this and make the necessary tension adjustments.

• Make sure all the threads can feed evenly off the spools. Uneven thread feeding can cause "hiccups" in your stitches. Some new spools of thread will feed unevenly at first until some of the thread is reeled off. If this is a problem, wind a bobbin from the spool with your sewing machine to eliminate the initial tightness.

• It looks great when you blend colors and mix types of thread. To change threads frequently, tie on the new thread and pull it through the guides. The knots on heavy thread won't fit through the eye of the loopers, so cut the knots off and use a threader. You can use just about any thread that will fit through the eye of the looper. Use the smaller diameter threads in the needles. The eye of the needle is too small for the heavier threads to feed through so use them in the loopers.

• Always use a smooth, even-textured thread or yarn (no bumps or bulges). Some of the bumps may be too large to pass through the eye of a looper and cause the thread to break or the machine to jam.

• Use good quality thread. Old or poor quality thread can break often, which means rethreading the serger and/or removing and repairing stitches. Many economy brands of thread have an irregular twist and can cause tension adjustment

problems. They also cause excess lint to build up in your machine, which can affect stitch quality. This can cause a lot of frustration and waste valuable time. Use good quality thread and save the bother.

• Buy enough thread to test serge and complete your project. It takes approximately five to ten yards of thread to test and set up the stitch and approximately ten yards of thread for each yard of serging. This amount will vary depending on the thread thickness, the stitch length, and the stitch width.

• Use a horizontal spool pin on the thread spindle when using metallic or Sliver threads. These types of threads need to feed off the spool without twisting, which can cause problems with breakage and fraying.

• Some threads, such as crochet thread and pearl cotton, are wound in a ball and won't feed off the thread spindle of the serger. Thread the serger first, then put the ball into a deep bowl or container that won't snag the thread. Set the container on the table or floor beside your serger. The ball of thread will need plenty of room to roll around as the thread feeds off. Unwind some of the thread into the bowl by hand if it doesn't feed evenly. The best way to use these types of thread is to wind them on an empty spool by hand or use an E-Z Winder.

• Some metallic threads may fray or break when used in the lower looper because there are more thread guides for the thread to go through. If this occurs, use a nonmetallic thread in the lower looper and metallic in the upper looper.

• Always use a press cloth to prevent touching the decorative threads with a hot iron. Nylon threads may melt with direct heat and other threads can be damaged or weakened by the soleplate of the iron. It's heartbreaking to finish the embellishments and then melt them off with the careless press of a hot iron.

SERGER STITCH SETTINGS

Project Title

Fabrics Used in Project

Stitch Type (select one)	Left Needle (LN)	Right Needle (RN)	Upper Looper (UL)	Lower Looper (LL)	Chain Stitch Looper (CSL)	Chain Stitch Needle (CSN)
Balanced Four-Thread Construction						
Balanced Three-Thread Construction						
Balanced Three-Thread Decorative						
Flatlock Two-Thread Flatlock Three-Thread						
Rolled Edge Two-Thread Rolled Edge Three-Thread						
Serger Chain Braid						
Chain Stitch						
Chain Stitch Braid						
Type of Thread						
Specialty Foot	Length		Width		Dif/F	

Attach a Stitch Sample to the Page

CHAPTER 6
Scrunched &Woven Vests

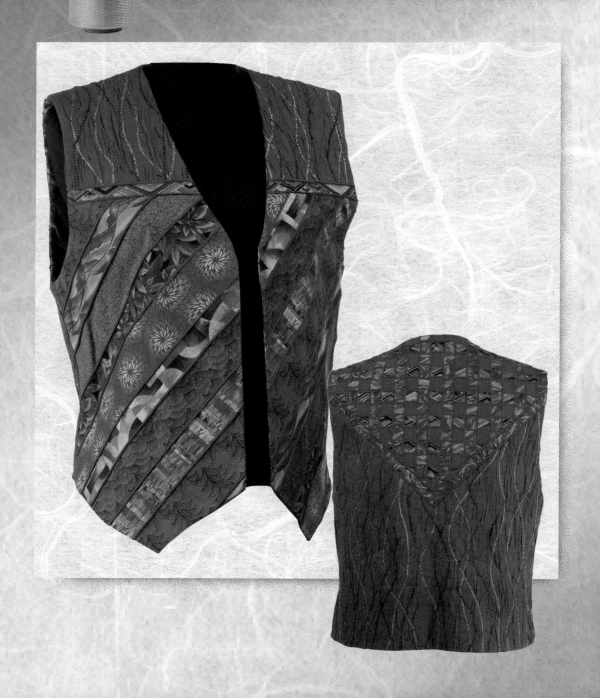

Materials

- your favorite vest pattern
- 1/4 to 1/3 yd each of 4 different fabrics
- 1 yd (depending on size and length of pattern) fabric to "scrunch" for the lower back and front yoke sections (1/4 yd of this fabric will be cut into strips for the Pintuck Patchwork)
- lining fabric - follow pattern recommendations
- underlining - same yardage as lining
- 2 yds fusible knit interfacing
- pattern tracing material or paper to make the front and back yokes
- variety of decorative serger threads to coordinate with fabrics for serger braid (30 or 40 wt. rayon, woolly nylon, metallic, acrylic, pearl rayon, ribbon floss, etc.)
- large spool 30 wt. rayon or woolly nylon for rolled hem and pintucks
- several spools polyester thread for needle when making braid
- Sulky invisible thread
- straight pins or T-pins and bodkin
- weaving board
- 2 yds 1/2"-wide paper-backed fusible web
- braid or couching foot and pintuck or piping foot for sewing machine (any foot with groove in bottom large enough to ride over serger chain braid and rolled edge)

The vest shown is the first garment I designed for a SergeArt class and has remained the most popular garment in my classes.

The design features serger chain braid stitched on scrunched fabric and woven yokes made from strips of fabric that have been serged with a rolled edge on both sides.

The pintuck fabric and weaving can be made with small amounts of fabric leftover from other garments. Use as many different fabrics as you want to make the pintuck fabric for the vest fronts. The width of the strips can vary. Serge together as many strips as needed to create fabric the length you need.

You can make a woven yoke and attach it to a ready-made garment. To make the pattern, place a piece of paper over the garment and trace the section to be covered with the yoke. Cover the raw edges with a rolled edge fabric strip.

Cutting

1 A Cut two vest front sections and one vest back from underlining as the base for stitching your serged fabric manipulations.

2 Cut one vest lining.

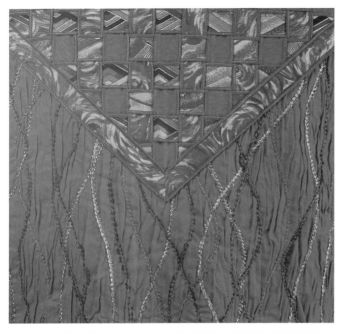

Serger Chain Braid

Make enough serger chain braid to stitch all over the scrunched fabric. The finished fabric will be used for the front yokes and the lower back. Refer to Chapter 4 for instructions on making serger chain braid.

Serger Chain Braid Setup: Three-Thread Rolled Edge

Follow the recommended stitch settings in your serger manual and set up for a three-thread rolled edge stitch to make serger chain braid. Start with a stitch length of 2. Set the needle tension at normal and set both of the looper tensions one number lower than the normal settings.

Thread both loopers with thick decorative thread and thread the needle with a finer thread. Experiment with the tensions and stitch length as you serge a couple of yards until the chain has the desired appearance.

Optional: For a five-thread serger, you can make some two-thread chain stitch braid to stitch on your garment. Follow instructions in Chapter 4 and in your manual to set up your machine for a two-thread chain stitch.

Measuring the Pattern

Measure the pattern pieces before cutting any fabric for the embellishments. Make the finished fabric several inches larger than the exact size needed.

Determining Yardage for Scrunching

1 Measure the longest distance of the lower back section (from where the back yoke ends to the bottom of the hem line edge). Include a seam allowance where the yoke and lower back sections overlap.

2 Measure the length of the front yoke from the shoulder seam to the seam that overlaps the pintuck fabric. Double this amount.

3 The larger of the two measurements will give the length you need for the finished scrunched fabric.

4 Measure the widest part of the lower back section (from side seam to side seam). Measure the widest part of the front yoke (from armscye to the front edge). Add three inches to the total for the width needed. (The suggested yardage is 2/3 to 3/4 yd fabric to use for scrunching, but your own measurements will give the exact amount needed.)

5 Cut fabric the length and width needed.

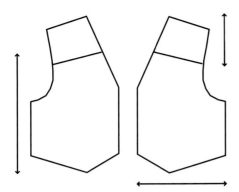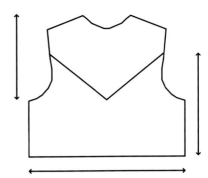

Measure the original pattern to determine yardage and make the patterns for the yoke sections.

Making the Yoke Patterns

Make a back and front yoke on paper from the vest pattern. Draw new pattern shapes for the yokes from the original pattern. When the pattern is cut into sections, add seam allowances where the sections need to overlap.

1 To make the V-shaped yoke for the vest back, place a mark on the pattern where you want the bottom point of the yoke to end. Make the yoke length proportionate to the vest length. Use the 45° angle line on your ruler and line it up along the place-on-fold line at the center back. Draw a line from the mark for the yoke bottom to the armscye.

2 Cut a piece of pattern tracing paper large enough to make a yoke pattern across the width of the entire the vest. Fold the paper in half. This lets you cut the finished woven fabric while it is flat instead of folded.

3 Lay the pattern on the paper, lining up the fold line of the pattern with the fold of the paper. Trace around the outside of the pattern. Draw the line for the bottom of the yoke on the paper.

4 Cut out the back yoke pattern.

5 Trace a pattern for the front yoke. The length of the front and back yokes should match at the armscyes. Make the length proportionate to the size of the vest pattern.

6 Cut out the front yoke pattern.

7 Use the back yoke pattern to cut the woven fabric and the front yoke pattern to cut the scrunched fabric.

Scrunched Fabric

Make the scrunched fabric, following the instructions in Chapter 4. Remember, it's better to have too much than not enough and any leftovers can be used in other projects.

Stitching Braid to the Scrunched Fabric

Sewing Machine: Zigzag Stitch

1 Set your machine for a medium width zigzag stitch. Use a braid, cording, or couching foot to guide the braid as it is stitched in place. Stitch some braid on a piece of practice fabric to set the length, width, and tension the way you want it. Set the stitch length at 2 and the stitch width between 2 and 3. Reduce the upper tension one or two numbers lower than the normal setting so the bobbin thread won't show on the right side.

2 Start on one edge of the scrunched fabric and "meander" to the other side of the fabric while stitching over the braid. Change colors of braid and top thread several times. There is no wrong way to do this. This is a freeform technique that releases you from any rules. Have a lot of fun!

3 Press the scrunched fabric from the wrong side, using a press cloth.

Cutting the Scrunched Fabric

1 Lay the underlining fabric with the back yoke pinned in place on top of the scrunched fabric. Leave enough room along one side of the fabric to cut out the front yokes. Cut out the scrunched fabric using the outline of the underlining as the pattern. It's better to cut the fabric when it's opened out flat instead of using the back pattern piece and cutting on a fold.

2 Place the front yoke pattern on the remaining scrunched fabric. Leave enough room to cut the second yoke. Add a 1/2″ seam allowance to allow for overlapping the sections. Cut two front yokes.

3 Place the cut out scrunched fabric for the lower back on top of the base fabric. Line up the edges. Lay the back yoke pattern in place on the upper back. Mark the lines for the V-shape on the scrunched fabric. Add a 1/2″ seam allowance to the scrunched fabric to allow for overlapping the sections. Remove the pattern and the base fabric. Trim the scrunched fabric on the marked line to fit the V-shape.

Woven Yoke

Cutting

Use four fabrics for weaving the back yoke. Cut all strips 1″-wide from selvage to selvage. The following recommendations are usually sufficient for the yoke. If making a yoke with a different pattern or size, cut more strips. The strips can also be wider if desired.

Size small or medium. Cut three 1″ x 44″ strips from each of the four fabrics (total 12 strips).

Size large and up. Cut four 1″ x 44″ strips from each of the four fabrics (total 16 strips).

Serger Setup: Two- or Three-Thread Rolled Edge

Follow the recommended stitch settings in your serger manual and set up for a two- or three-thread rolled edge. Use a short stitch length (1 to 1½) and adjust to your preference. Test your stitch settings and adjust them while serging one layer of fabric.

For a two-thread stitch, use decorative thread in the lower looper and matching polyester thread in the needle. For a three-thread stitch, use decorative thread in the upper looper, matching decorative or polyester thread in the lower looper, and matching polyester thread in the needle.

Serging

❶ Serge a rolled edge along one side of all the 1″ strips. Keep the right side of the fabric facing up. Chain the strips together as you serge.

❷ When you finish one side of all the strips, turn the chained strips around and start from the end of the last strip you serged. Serge the other side of the strips with the right side of the fabric up. This keeps the top side of the rolled edge stitching consistently on the right side of the fabric.

❸ Using a press cloth, press the strips from the wrong side.

Weaving

1 Cut interfacing for the back yoke 1″ larger than the pattern all the way around. You will cut it to size after making the woven fabric.

2 Pin the interfacing fusible-side-up to a weaving board.

3 Choose two fabrics from the 1″-wide rolled edge strips to place vertically and two to place horizontally for weaving.

4 Pin the vertical strips alternately in place right-side-up on top of the interfacing. Place the first vertical strip centered in the middle and work out to the sides. Place the strips close together without gaps between them. Trim each strip after pinning it in place. The length of all the strips must extend to the edges of the interfacing.

5 Weave the horizontal strips right-side-up, alternating over and under the vertical strips. Pin in place and trim as you go. Be sure to close any gaps between the strips. Use a ruler to check that the strips are straight.

6 When you have everything lined up and pinned in place, use a press cloth and fuse the strips to the interfacing. Start pressing from the middle and fuse out to the edges. Don't slide the iron over the fabric, just set the iron straight down on the fabric, fuse, then pick it straight up. Move the iron and repeat.

7 Remove the pins when everything is well fused.

8 Place the back yoke pattern on the right side of the woven fabric, lined up with the center strip, and cut out.

Lay the pattern on the right side of the finished yoke to cut.

The wrong side of the woven yoke fused to iron-on knit interfacing.

Pintuck Fabric

Pattern Layout

View 1

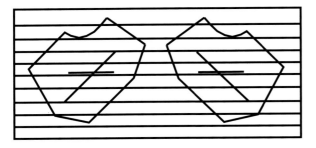

The chevron design will point up

View 2

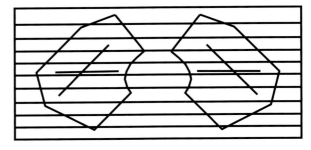

The chevron will point down

View 3

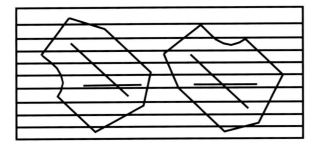

The strips are on the diagonal

View 4

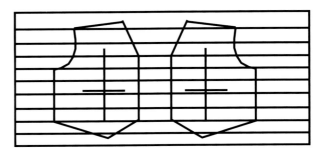

The strips go straight across

There are several different ways to layout and cut the vest front. See the suggested cutting layout views #1-4 for pattern placement. Decide which angle you want to use before measuring to determine the length of fabric to make.

Measuring the Vest Front Pattern

❶ Mark two lines on the pattern in each direction on a 45° angle to the grain line. These will help you lay out the pattern on the finished pintuck fabric more accurately.

❷ Measure the length of the pattern for the vest front, from the bottom of the front yoke to the hem line. Add a 1/2″ seam allowance to underlap the front yoke. Be sure to add 1/4″ seam allowances on both sides for each strip.

❸ Measure the widest part of the vest front.

For layouts #1, #2, and #3, measure the distance from the vest hem to the front yoke at a 45° angle to the grain line.

For layout #4, measure the length of the vest front from the yoke to the hem. It must be as wide as both the front sections.

Cutting the Strips for Pintuck Fabric

Cut enough strips to make fabric long enough for the layout you chose for cutting the vest fronts. Ten 2½″ x 44″ strips make a finished piece of pintuck fabric approximately 22″ x 44″.

For sizes XL and over, make two pieces of pintuck fabric. Cut a vest front from each piece. Don't use the entire 44″ width of the strips. Cut them the width needed before constructing the pintuck fabric.

Serger Setup: Two- or Three-Thread Rolled Edge

Continue using the rolled edge setting on your serger. Follow the recommended stitch settings in your manual. Use the same stitch length and width you used for the woven strips.

Thread your serger with the color you want to use for the pintuck patchwork. Test your stitch settings and adjust by serging two layers of fabric.

Serging

1 Arrange the fabric strips in the order you want them. The most visible strips of the pintuck fabric will be in the middle so place your favorite fabrics in the center area. Using a rolled edge stitch, serge the strips wrong-sides-together two at a time. Don't trim the fabric.

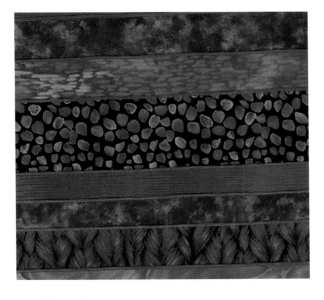

2 When all the strips are serged into pairs, serge the pairs together two at a time. This helps to minimize stretching and distortion. Always start serging from the same end each time so the top side of the stitching will be consistently on the same side of the fabric.

3 Continue serging all the sets of strips together two at a time until the fabric is completed.

4 Using a press cloth, press the pintucks in the same direction with the top side of the stitches showing.

Cutting the Pintuck Fabric

1 Lay the pattern on the fabric, following the layout you chose, with the pressed tucks pointing to the bottom of the vest.

2 Place the pattern pieces with the bottom edge and the underarm/side seam point lining up along the same strips. Make sure both sides of the front will fit on the fabric before cutting.

3 Cut the front vest sections one layer at a time.

Putting It All Together

Sewing Machine: Straight Stitch

1 Use a straight machine stitch to sew each fabric manipulation section to the base fabric. Pin all the embellished sections in place and straight stitch through the overlapping layers and around the outside edges. Make sure the strips along the edges of the yoke remain even and don't shift as you stitch over them. Lay the patterns back on the finished vest sections and trim if necessary.

2 Use a strip leftover from the weaving to cover the overlapping seam allowances of the embellished sections. Iron a narrow strip of fusible web on the back of the weaving strips to cover the raw edges where the sections overlap. Sew or fold a miter in the back yoke strip before fusing it. Fuse the strips in place centered over the raw edge.

3 Sew the strips in place with a straight stitch on your sewing machine. Use a pintuck foot, piping foot, or a foot with a groove in the bottom for the rolled edge to slide through and it will be easier to stitch close to the serged edge. The sewing machine needle should come down into the fabric right next to the needle line of the rolled edge stitching and not through the looper thread. Use clear monofilament nylon thread so the stitching line won't show.

Right: The pink scrunched vest was made by Dena Burns, Houston.

Final Garment Construction

Follow the instructions in Chapter 4 for final vest construction on the serger or use your favorite method.

Serger Setup: Balanced Four-Thread Construction Stitch

Set up the serger for a balanced four-thread construction stitch. Use polyester thread in the needles and loopers. Test the stitch settings and adjust by serging four layers of fabric.

Variation of the scrunched and woven vest.

Variation: Jennifer's Vest

My daughter wanted me to make her a SergeArt vest as a Christmas present. I handed her Judy Murrah's *Jacket Jazz* books for inspiration. The garment that caught her attention was the "Spring has Sprung" vest from *More Jazz*. She liked the use of the wedge ruler to cut the fabric, but she wanted me to use a flatlock stitch instead of the rolled edge to serge the wedges. She really loves the scrunched fabric and woven yoke of my first SergeArt vest, so I incorporated them into her vest as well. She graciously let me borrow it back to be photographed.

Some of the techniques on this vest are the same as the main vest featured in this chapter, but the embellishment placement is different. I used a medium wedge ruler to cut the fabric for the lower back and one side of the front. The fabric wedges were flatlocked together with the loops showing. The other side of the front was made from scrunched fabric with serger chain braid. The front and back yokes were made from woven rolled edge fabric strips.

There are many types of rulers available to use for cutting fabric into various shapes. You can serge the fabric back together using your choice of a rolled edge, flatlock, or balanced three-thread decorative stitch. Serger braid was twisted into a large cord and couched on the vest to cover where the sections overlapped.

CHAPTER 7

Patchwork Wrap-Around Skirt & Vest

Materials

- Woodstock pattern by Park Bench Patterns (or similar pattern)
- 3 yds total various fabrics for skirt (follow pattern recommendations)
- 1¾ yds total various fabrics for top
- 500-yard spool 30-wt. Sulky thread for upper looper
- cone woolly nylon for lower looper
- cone polyester serger thread for needle (all thread should match)
- 2 buttons or frog closures for vest

The patchwork skirt and vest was made using the Woodstock Pattern from Park Bench Patterns and features a rolled edge stitch. It was made from a stack of various hand-dyed cotton fabrics by Hoffman and Lee Anne's Batiks from my stash that I was just itching to use. It's great fun to mix and match fabrics for this type of garment. I used 15 different fabrics for both garments. This type of outfit is suitable for cottons but also looks great made from rayon fabrics. The look is quite different, depending on the fabric choice. I plan to make another one using lace fabrics to be worn over leggings.

Both garments are asymmetrical in design. The vest has various angles along the hem and an offset front closure. It can be worn open or closed. The wrap-around skirt has an uneven hem and ties at the waist. Let the vest hang open with a top underneath or add your favorite type of closure.

This pattern is roughly a size 14 but can be easily adjusted for a larger or smaller size. The size of the skirt is determined by where you place the tie at the waist. It's especially important to measure this type of pattern before cutting out any fabric. If the vest needs to be larger, simply extend the side seams or the length. I'm way past the point of letting my midriff show, so I added 4″ to the length of the vest. I also added some width to the side seams.

This technique is suitable for many garment styles. Use a pattern with simple lines that can be made from a single layer of fabric without facings, interfacing, or turned hems.

Cut the seam allowances down to 1/4″ on all pattern pieces. The pieced sections will fit together more easily than if trimming a 5/8″ seam allowance with the serger.

Many different types of thread can be used for the rolled edge. Match the weight of the thread to the weight of the fabric for best results.

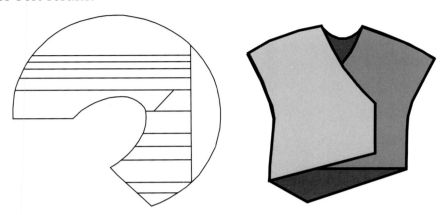

Sections for the wrap-around skirt.

Layout & Cutting

If using your choice of a similar pattern, divide the pattern into various sections to duplicate the look of this garment. Number the sections with a sewing order to aid in serging the pieces together.

❶ Cut out all sections for the skirt. The sections can be cut on either the lengthwise or crossgrain, depending on the length of the pattern section. Some of the sections are almost two yards long. These can be pieced or cut in a continuous strip with the lengthwise grain of the fabric. Add 1/4″ seam allowances where the pieced sections will join.

❷ To help remember the correct sewing order, keep the pattern piece on each section until needed.

❸ *Optional: Mark lines on the pattern for the vest to divide it into sections. Add 1/4″ seam allowances where the pieced sections will join.*

❹ Cut the vest from several different fabrics. Cut each side of the front and the back from a single layer of fabric. (Asymmetrical designs aren't usually cut on double layers of fabric or on a fold.)

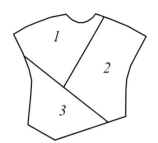

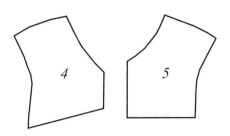

Serge together following the numbered stitching order

Vest pattern cut into sections

Putting It All Together
Serger Setup: Three-Thread Rolled Edge

Follow the recommended stitch settings in your manual and set up the serger for a three-thread rolled edge stitch. A three-thread stitch is stronger than the two-thread for garment construction.

Thread the serger with Sulky 30-wt. thread in the upper looper. Use matching woolly nylon thread in the lower looper and polyester thread in the right needle.

Use a stitch length of 1½ to 2 and adjust to your preference. Don't set the stitch length too short or it may perforate the fabric too closely and weaken the fibers at the seamline. Set the stitch width a little wider than your manual suggests for a rolled edge. Letting a little more fabric "roll" into the stitch will add strength to the seam. Test your stitch settings and adjust them while serging two layers of fabric.

Serging

❶ Serge all the skirt sections with the fabric wrong-sides-together. Trim loose threads off the edge of the fabric while serging, but don't trim any fabric (uneven trimming will cause the fabric to ripple). Follow the stitching order suggested in the pattern instructions to serge the sections together.

❷ Serge around the outer edges of the skirt with a rolled edge for the hem.

❸ Serge the fabric wrong-sides-together to join the cut apart sections for the vest. Serge these sections wrong-sides-together to finish construction.

❹ Serge around the outer edges of the vest with a rolled edge for the hem. Follow the pattern instructions for finishing the skirt waistband.

CHAPTER 8
Peek-a-Boo Pleats
Jacket & Blouse

Peek-a-Boo Pleats Blouse made by Carol McKinney, Houston.

Peek-a-Boo Pleats Jacket made by Carol McKinney, Houston.

Materials

- jacket or blouse pattern (see below for pattern suggestions)
- main fabric (measure pattern)
- coordinating fabric (measure pattern)
- lining (follow pattern recommendations) optional for blouse
- 2 large spools decorative serger thread to coordinate with main fabric (rayon or woolly nylon threads work well for this technique)
- 2 cones matching polyester thread for needle and lower looper
- Sulky invisible thread or coordinating thread for bartacks
- straight pins or small safety pins
- iron-on stabilizer or freezer paper
- 1″-wide masking tape

This jacket and blouse were made by my friend Carol McKinney. She is well known for her beautiful cutwork and appliqué patterns and for her prize-winning garments in the Sulky Challenges and Sulky books. She is also quite talented at the serger. I feel very privileged to share Carol's wonderfully serged garments with you.

Carol used the Kimono Jacket pattern by Judy Bishop Designs for the jacket. It has batwing type sleeves and a one-piece yoke that goes across the shoulders from sleeve hem to sleeve hem. There is a lot of room on the yoke for additional embellishments of your choice. The blouse was made from a basic pattern that features a front and back yoke. (For more examples of jackets made in class by the "Material Girls", see page 96-97.)

This technique is similar to hanging wallpaper in that the design of the main fabric needs to match after the fabric is serged back together. It's not hard to do this technique, but it does takes some planning and you have to pay close attention when cutting and laying out the fabric.

Pattern Selection and Where to Use Peek-a-Boo Fabric

Here are some suggestions for selecting a pattern for the peek-a-boo pleats technique and what sections should be made from the pleated fabric.

Choose a pattern with few pieces - this technique works best when the pattern sections are large.

Choose the pattern before buying the fabric. Measure the pattern pieces for the correct yardage.

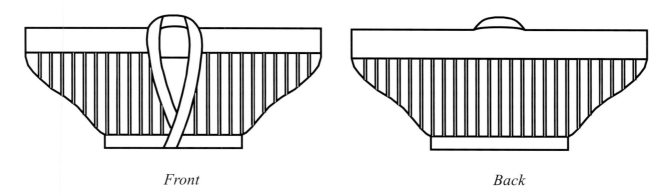

Front   *Back*

Peek-a-Boo Jacket made from Kimono Jacket pattern by Judy Bishop Designs.

For a Jacket

If the sleeve and body of the jacket are one piece, make pleated fabric for the entire jacket, sleeves included. If the sleeve and body of the jacket are two pieces, make pleated fabric for the body of the jacket only. Use plain fabric or another type of embellishment for the sleeves.

For a Blouse

Choose a blouse pattern with a separate front and back yoke. Use peek-a-boo pleats for the body of the blouse and plain fabric or another type of embellishment for the yokes (rolled edge pintucks are on the sample garment). Make plain sleeves from the main fabric.

Measure the Pattern to Determine Yardage

Measure the length and width of the pattern pieces that will be cut from the pleated fabric. Add 4″ to the total for each pattern. Unless the pattern pieces are very wide, you will need two times the length of the garment (plus 8″) and the sleeve length. Add the totals to determine the amount of yardage needed. You will need 1½ times more of the coordinating fabric than the main print for the front and back. This fabric is not used for the sleeves. If the pattern pieces are wide, you will need extra yardage.

Fabric Selection

When selecting fabric, choose a main fabric with a scene or design. The main fabric will be cut apart into 2″-wide strips and serged back together with 3″-wide strips of the coordinating fabric between them. You may have to buy extra yardage if the fabric has a definite picture or scene that you want to have in a specific place on the garment. You may also need to match the scene from front to back, depending on your choice of fabric.

Use a solid or tone-on-tone coordinating fabric for the inside of the pleats. Two fabrics with distinct prints would get too busy when the pleats open up and the "boos" are peeking at you. For a variation, you can use several different colors of fabrics and alternate them for the pleats.

Use fabrics that are compatible and of similar weight. Lightweight fabric will stretch more as the strips are serged together and will cause distortion of the scene you are re-creating.

Choose fabrics that can withstand the heat of the iron when pressing the pleats.

Cutting Strips for the Pleated Fabric

Cut the print fabric in lengthwise strips, keeping them in order. Serge them back together by inserting a pleat strip of a more subdued fabric between each print strip. Fold the pleat strip to bring the print fabric back together. Keep the strips in sequence so they will fit back together in the original print pattern.

Cut all the strips from the main and coordinating fabrics the same length for each pattern section. This will help you line up the strips when serging them together from opposite directions. Your final design will be aligned when all the strips are serged.

❶ If the main fabric has a definite scene, place the pattern on the fabric to see where the print design falls. Decide what part of the print you want to use. Measure the length and width of the front and back pattern pieces. Add 4″ to the total. Cut enough sections of fabric for each of the pattern pieces (see Tip).

TIP
If the front and back pattern pieces are close to the same length, cut the fabric for them the same length. This will allow you to cut all the coordinating fabric used for the pleats the same length, using less yardage. You won't use more fabric than 1½ times the main print.

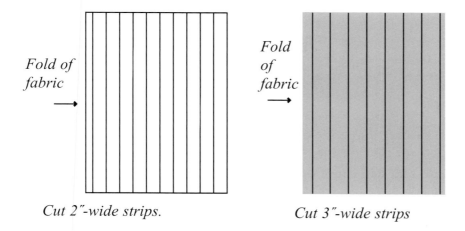

Fold of fabric →

Fold of fabric →

Cut 2″-wide strips.

Cut 3″-wide strips

Cut the first strip on the fold and keep the strips in order.

❷ Cut the main print into 2″-wide strips the length of the pattern (*not across the selvage*). Keep these strips in the order they were cut. Cut the strips starting from the center fold. This will keep the print design in order without causing a break in the design. Discard the selvage strips when the width is under 2″.

❸ It's very important to follow this step carefully. To keep the strips in order, start with the top strip nearest the selvage. Pick up the top strip and place it to the side, leaving the strip underneath untouched for the moment. Then pick up the next strip on top and lay it down beside the first. The prints from these two strips should fit together. Continue this process until you get to the folded center strip. Place it next to the others, then lay out the strips that are wrong-side-up next to where the folded center strip was. Continue laying the strips out in sequential order. When you're done, the strips should be in a single layer, face-up, in the same pattern as before they were cut.

❹ Cut sections of coordinating fabric for the pleats the same length as needed for each of the pattern pieces from the main fabric. Since the pleated strips are wider than the ones from the main fabric, cut an extra length of fabric to have enough strips to make all the pleats (unless you used the technique in the Tip). Cut the fabric for the pleats into 3″-wide strips. These strips don't have to be kept in order.

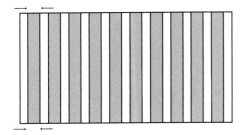

Bring the rolled edge seams of the 2″-wide strips together and center them over the 3″-wide strips, forming a pleat.

Serging the Pleated Fabric
Serger Setup: Three-Thread Rolled Edge

Follow the recommended stitch settings in your manual and set up the serger for a three-thread rolled edge stitch. Thread the serger with decorative thread in the upper looper and matching polyester thread in the lower looper and right needle. If using woolly nylon thread, put it in both loopers.

Use a short stitch length of 1 to 1½ and adjust to your preference. Set the stitch width a little wider than your manual suggests for a rolled edge. Letting a little more fabric "roll" into the stitch will add strength to the seam. Test your stitch settings and adjust them while serging two layers of fabric.

Serge the strips wrong-sides-together, with the main print *always* as the strip on top. The coordinating fabric should be on the bottom facing the feed dogs. You will alternate the stitching direction each time a strip is added, so the top side of the rolled edge should be on the right side of the main print fabric.

Ironing the Pleats and Marking the Fabric

❶ Lay the fabric right-side-up on a large ironing surface. Bring the strips of the main print together, centering the rolled edges over the pleat strips.

❷ Using pins that won't melt when ironed, pin the pleats one at a time, then iron. Pin the pleats in place at 6″ intervals. Begin measuring 3″ from the top for the first pleat. Begin 6″ from the top for the next pleat. Repeat until the fabric is pleated and pinned for bartack placement. For smaller sizes, make the intervals closer. You will later stitch the bartacks at each pin placement to hold the pleats together.

❸ Slide a large piece of iron-on stabilizer under the pleated fabric, with the fusible side to the wrong side of the fabric (or use freezer paper, shiny side toward the wrong side of the fabric). The stabilizer keeps the pleats from shifting when sewing the bartacks.

❹ Use masking tape to tape the pleated fabric to the stabilizer along the outer edges of the fabric.

❺ Flip the fabric and stabilizer over so the fabric is face down on the ironing surface. Press the stabilizer to the fabric with a medium heat setting.

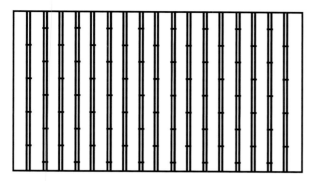

Bartack placement

Fabric for the Peek-a-Boo Jacket by Mary Nell Johnson, Houston.

Sewing Machine Setup

1 Set up the sewing machine to make a bartack. Set the stitch length to zero so the fabric doesn't move. The width should be set so the needle enters the fabric on either side of the rolled edges.

2 Stitch the bartacks at the marks or pins. Alternate the placement of the bartacks on every other pleat.

3 Remove the stabilizer and press the fabric again.

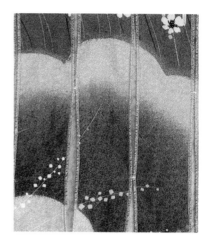

Yoke Embellishments

Rolled Edge Pintucks

Use the standard rolled edge setting and a stitch length of 1½ to 2. Because the tucks are bulky, the satin stitch setting won't work.

This technique works best on light to medium weight fabrics. Don't try to match up the pintucks at the seamlines, they usually don't line up evenly when sewing the seams together. Instead, use an asymmetrical placement for the pintucks. Mark the placement lines for tucks. Fold and press the fabric wrong-sides-together. Serge the pintucks without cutting the fabric, using a lightweight decorative thread in the upper looper.

Seminole Patchwork

The Kimono Jacket pattern includes instructions for making a Seminole yoke. Other sources for Seminole designs are listed in the Bibliography.

Embellishment Choices Include:
  • Free motion or machine embroidery on plain fabric or on top of the patchwork fabric.
  • Decorative stitching (this is a great place to use those fancy stitches on your sewing machine).
  • Patchwork.
  • Appliqué. There are many great books and patterns on appliqué. This is a great place to put that new design you have been wanting to do.

Embroidered fabric for the Peek-a-Boo Jacket yoke by Mary Nell Johnson, Houston.

Putting It All Together

Peek-a-Boo Pleats Jacket with Seminole patchwork yoke made by Sabrina Szymczyk, Houston.

Peek-a-Boo Pleats Jacket with embroidered Seminole patchwork yoke made by Jo Largent, Houston.

Cutting the Pleated Fabric

Lay the pattern piece on the pleated fabric, lining up any designs that should match at the side seams. Center the edges of the pattern so the thickness of the rolled edge stitching doesn't get included in the garment seam allowances.

Sewing Machine: Straight Stitch

Set your sewing machine on straight stitch and sew around the outer edges of the cut fabric to keep the pleats from shifting during construction.

Final Garment Construction

Follow pattern instructions for final garment construction. The Kimono Jacket pattern is well suited to be constructed mostly on the serger. Use 1/2″ seam allowances for this pattern.

Lining is optional. If not using a lining, serge all raw edges before constructing the garment on the sewing machine.

Serger Setup: Balanced Four-Thread Construction Stitch

Set up the serger for a balanced four-thread construction stitch. Use polyester thread in the needles and loopers. Test the stitch settings and adjust by serging four layers of fabric.

CHAPTER 9

Las Vegas Jacket

Materials

- Buy extra fabric for larger sizes. All yardages are approximate.
- pattern - Tuxedo jacket #8 from *Jacket Jazz Encore* by Judy Murrah (or similar jacket pattern)
- lining fabric - follow pattern recommendations (You'll need an extra yard if you want to use it in weaving and for front. See below.)
- underlining - same amount as lining
- 1 yd fabric - same amount as lining for weaving and front (I used multi-colored stripe)
- 1/4 yd each of 4 coordinating solid color fabrics (I used Cherrywood fabrics)
- 1/2 yd each of 2 medium print fabrics (I used butterfly print and green/yellow/orange/blue leaf print)
- 1⅔ yd fabric for strips in front, cuff, lapel, and back
- pattern tracing material or paper large enough to trace back yoke
- fusible knit interfacing
- pair shoulder pads - 3/8″ to 3/4″ thick
- 12-15 yds 3/8″-wide ribbon
- assorted glass beads for back
- decorative serger threads to coordinate with fabrics for serger braid - 30 or 40 wt. rayon, woolly nylon, metallic, acrylic, pearl rayon, ribbon floss, Decor 6, pearl cotton, candlelight
- large spool 30 wt. rayon thread for flatlock stitching
- Sulky thread - rayon, metallic, sliver, Sulky invisible thread
- 4 cones matching polyester thread
- T-pins and bodkin
- weaving board
- braid or couching foot for sewing machine (any foot with groove in bottom large enough to ride over serger chain braid)

This jacket was made to enter in the Pfaff Dealer Convention Fashion Show held in Las Vegas. It was later featured in the Pfaff Club Magazine #17.

My daughter went to modeling school but I was the one who had to model it for the fashion show. I am not the "runway model" type and there is nothing worse than seeing your rear end displayed on a huge screen right in front of you as you leave the runway. I much prefer to make the garments.

It began with a stack of beautifully colorful fabrics that were calling to me from a shelf. I had to figure out what to do with them, so I went to Judy Murrah's *Jacket Jazz* books for inspiration on techniques I could adapt to the serger. The back yoke and the sleeves were the result. The front of the jacket was made by flatlocking strips of fabric and the lapels and lower back were made from scrunched fabric with couched-on serger chain braid.

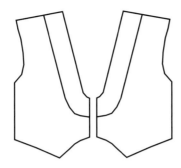

Flatlocked fabric for fronts, scrunched fabric for lapels

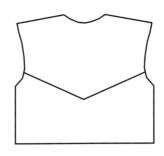

Woven yoke, scrunched fabric for lower back

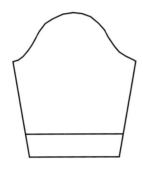

Patchwork fabric for sleeves, flatlocked fabric for cuffs

Tuxedo Jacket pattern by Judy Murrah

Cutting

❶ Cut two fronts, two sleeves, and one back from the underlining as a base for stitching your serged fabric manipulations.

❷ Cut one lining.

Measuring the Pattern

Measure the pattern pieces before cutting any fabric for the embellishments. Make the finished fabric several inches larger than the exact size needed.

Making Serger Chain Braid

Make enough serger chain braid to stitch all over the scrunched fabric. The finished fabric will be used for the front lapels and the lower back. Refer to Chapter 4 for full instructions on making serger chain braid.

Serger Setup: Three-Thread Rolled Edge

Follow the recommended stitch settings in your manual and set up the serger for a three-thread rolled edge stitch to make serger chain braid. Thread both loopers with thick decorative thread and use a finer thread for the needle.

Start with a stitch length of 2. Set the needle tension at normal and set both of the looper tensions one number lower than the normal settings. Experiment with the tensions and stitch length as you serge a couple of yards until the chain has the desired appearance.

Optional: For a five-thread serger, you can also make some two-thread chain stitch braid to stitch on your garment. Follow instructions in Chapter 2 and in your manual to set up for a two-thread chain stitch.

Yardage for Scrunching

Scrunched fabric with couched serger braid is used for the lower back and lapels.

❶ To determine yardage, measure the longest distance of the lower back section from where the back yoke ends to the bottom of the hem line edge. Include a seam allowance where the yoke and lower back sections overlap.

❷ Measure the length of the front lapels and double the amount. The larger of the two measurements is the length of finished scrunched fabric you need.

❸ Measure the widest part of the lower back section (from side seam to side seam). Measure the widest part of the lapels. Add 3″ to the total for the width needed. (The recommendation is to have 2/3 to 3/4 yd of fabric to use for scrunching, but your own measurements will give the exact amount needed.)

❹ Cut the fabric the length and width needed.

Making the Scrunched Fabric

Make the scrunched fabric following the instructions in Chapter 4. Remember that it's better to have too much than not enough and any leftovers can be used in other projects.

Stitching Braid to the Scrunched Fabric

❶ Set your sewing machine for a medium width zigzag stitch. Use a braid, cording, or couching foot to guide the braid as it is stitched in place. Practice stitching some braid on a piece of fabric to find the length, width, and tension setup for the look you want. Set the stitch length at 2 and the stitch width between 2 and 3. Reduce the upper tension 1 to 2 numbers below the normal setting so the bobbin thread doesn't show on the right side.

❷ Start on one edge of the scrunched fabric and "meander" to the other side of the fabric while stitching over the braid. Change colors of braid and top thread several times. There is no wrong way to do this. This is a freeform technique that releases you from any rules. Have a lot of fun!

❸ Use a press cloth and press the scrunched fabric from the wrong side.

Cutting the Scrunched Fabric

❶ Lay the back underlining fabric on top of the scrunched fabric. Leave room along one side to cut out two lapels. Cut out the lower jacket back from the scrunched fabric. Use the outline of the base fabric as the pattern.

❷ Place the lapel pattern on the fabric where you like the design and cut. Be sure to flip the pattern over when you cut the second piece.

❸ Place the cut out back section of the scrunched fabric on top of the base fabric, lining it up along the edges. Add a seam allowance to overlap the sections. Cut out a wedge from the scrunched fabric to follow the shape of the yoke. Cover this raw edge with a leftover 1″ strip.

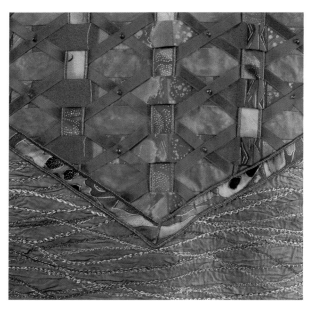

Back Yoke

The back yoke for this jacket was made from a technique called "Woven String Strips" in Judy Murrah's book *More Jazz.* Refer to the instructions in Chapter 6 for making a woven yoke as an alternative.

You will need to make several 1″-wide rolled edge weaving strips to complete the yoke.

❶ Make a pattern for the back yoke.

❷ Cut eight strips 1½″-wide from two different fabrics (16 strips total). Trim them to the length needed to go across the upper back of the jacket.

❸ Sew the strips together on the sewing machine, leaving a 1″ evenly spaced opening every 2″ to weave the rolled edge strips through. Sew for 2″, skip over 1″, sew 2″ more, and skip again until you reach the end of the strip.

④ Weave the rolled edge strips through the 1″ openings.

⑤ Weave the ribbon in a diamond pattern through the 1″ strips. I sewed the beads on by sewing machine in the intersections of the ribbon.

Cutting

The fabric for the front right side is made from two fabrics cut into 1½″-wide strips (from the lining fabric and the large piece of solid fabric also used for scrunching).

① Cut enough 1½″-wide strips from two different fabrics to make flatlocked fabric the length and width of the jacket right front.

Serge 1½″-wide strips together, cut into 3½″ squares

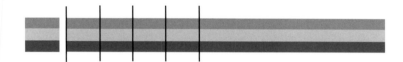

② The fabric for the front left side and the sleeves is made from 3½″ squares. Some of the strips are pieced together before cutting them into squares. Cut all the required yardage into 3½″ squares at the same time

③ Cut three or four 3½″-wide strips from the two other print fabrics. Cut the strips into 3½″ squares.

Sleeves

Use 3½″ squares to make fabric for the sleeves. Do the patchwork on the sewing machine or serger (the seams are inside because flatlocking snags easily on the sleeves). Use leftover flatlocked strips on the cuffs. Use a balanced four-thread construction stitch if you serge the squares together. You don't need the entire length on the sleeve. The cuff is made from leftover flatlocked strips used on the front. Make the cuff length proportionate to the sleeve length.

Serger Setup: Balanced Four-Thread Construction Stitch

Set up the serger for a balanced four-thread construction stitch. Use polyester thread in the needles and loopers. Test the stitch settings and adjust by serging two layers of fabric.

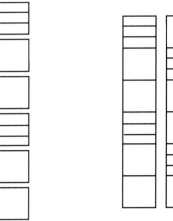
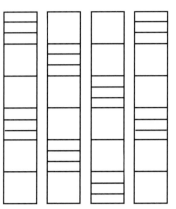
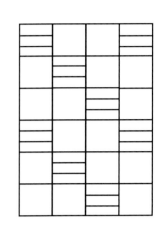

Arrange the squares in the desired layout

Serge the squares into strips

Serge the strips together to finish the fabric

Use the 3½″ squares from the print fabrics and arrange them with the pieced squares to make two pieces of fabric large enough for the sleeve length, minus the cuff length. Serge the squares together into strips the length needed. Serge the strips together to make the final fabric.

Flatlocking the Fronts

Serger Setup: Two- or Three-Thread Flatlock

Follow the recommended stitch settings in your manual to adjust your serger for a two- or three-thread flatlock stitch. Use the left needle and adjust to a wide stitch width. Start with a stitch length of 1 to 2 and adjust to your preference. The needle tension should be loose enough to allow the seam to open flat. Test and adjust your stitches on two layers of fabric.

For a three-thread stitch, place the decorative thread in the upper looper. Use polyester thread in the needle and polyester or woolly nylon thread in the lower looper. For a two-thread stitch, place decorative thread in the lower looper and polyester thread in the needle.

Serging: Constructing the Flatlocked Fabric

Left Front

1️⃣ Arrange the 3½″ squares in the order you want them.

2️⃣ Flatlock the squares wrong-sides-together. Open each seam before adding another square. Start serging from the same end each time.

3️⃣ When all the squares are serged into strips the length of the front, serge the strips together.

4️⃣ Continue serging until the fabric is the size needed.

5️⃣ Press from the back, using a press cloth. You now have finished fabric for the left front side.

Right Front

1️⃣ Arrange the 1½″ strips for the right front side.

2️⃣ Flatlock the strips wrong-sides-together. Open each seam before adding another strip. Start serging from the same end each time.

3️⃣ Continue serging until the fabric is the size needed.

4️⃣ Press from the back, using a press cloth. You now have finished fabric for right front side.

Putting It All Together

Cutting

1️⃣ Place the woven fabric on the cutting table weaving-side-up. Lay the back yoke pattern in place, lining it up with the center strip and cut away the excess fabric.

2️⃣ Cut the sleeves from the patchwork fabrics.

3️⃣ Cut the fronts from the finished flatlock fabrics.

Stitching

Sewing Machine: Straight Stitch

1️⃣ Stitch each fabric manipulation section to the underlining. Pin all the embellished sections in place and straight stitch through the overlapping layers and around the outside edges.

Adjust the needle position of your sewing machine to straight stitch right next to the needle thread of the rolled edge to attach the strip.

Make sure the strips along the edges of the yoke remain even and don't shift as you stitch over them. Check to see that everything is attached and in the right place before you continue. Lay the patterns back on the finished vest sections and trim if necessary.

❷ Use a leftover weaving strip to cover the raw edges of the back yoke. Iron a narrow strip of fusible web on the back of the weaving strip to cover the raw edge where the sections overlap. Fold or sew a miter to the back yoke strip before fusing it. Fuse it in place centered over the seam allowance. Sew it with a straight stitch on your sewing machine. Use a pintuck foot, piping foot, or a foot with a groove in the bottom for the rolled edge to slide through and it will be easier to stitch close to the serged edge. The sewing machine needle should come down in the fabric right next to the needle line of the rolled edge stitching and not through the looper thread. Use clear monofilament nylon or Sulky invisible thread so the stitching line will barely show.

Final Garment Construction
Serger Setup: Balanced Four-Thread Construction Stitch

Follow the pattern instructions for final garment construction. Use polyester thread in the needles and loopers. Set a wide stitch width and a stitch length of 2½. Test your stitch settings and adjust by serging through four layers of fabric.

CHAPTER 10

Flatlocked Patchwork Vest

Vest made by Dena Burns, Houston.

Materials

- your favorite vest pattern
- 1/4 to 1/3 yd each of 5 different cotton fabrics
- fabric - length of the vest back in 1 of the 5 above
- lining fabric - follow pattern recommendations
- underlining - same yardage as lining

- 2 spools decorative serger thread to coordinate with fabrics (rayon, woolly nylon, metallic, etc.)
- 2 cones matching polyester thread for needle and lower looper
- Sulky invisible thread
- 1 yd Sulky Totally Stable Iron On Stabilizer

This vest was designed as a simple and easy SergeArt project featuring the flatlock stitch. It goes together very quickly and is a great first project for making wearable art on your serger.

Always use the widest stitch width for flatlocking woven fabrics so the seam doesn't ravel. Quilt piecing is done on woven fabrics using 1/4″ seam allowances and the seams hold, so if you use at least a 1/4″ seam allowance for flatlocking, the seams won't come out.

Don't flatlock woven fabrics to construct seams that will bear the weight of the garment. The stress on construction seams may pull the stitching out. Flatlocking on woven fabrics is best suited for piecing "nonstressed" areas. A balanced four-thread construction stitch should be used for the weight-bearing seams.

Cutting

1 Cut the underlining as a base for your serged fabric.
2 Cut the vest lining. Follow the layout for the vest pattern.
3 Cut one vest back.

Measuring the Pattern

To be more efficient with time and materials, measure the length and width of the pattern. Refer to Chapter 1 for information on measuring your pattern to determine yardage. Make the flatlocked fabric 2″ larger than the exact size needed.

Cutting the Strips

Cut enough strips to make fabric the length of the vest front. Add in a 1/4″ seam allowance on both sides of each strip.

The following measurements will make a finished piece or flatlock fabric approximately 31″ wide x 35″ long after cutting six 1″ strips used for the vest back. The measurements given will make two vest fronts up to 15½″ wide x 35″ long.

If your pattern is wider, skip the step on cutting the strips for the back. To embellish the back, use strips leftover after cutting the fronts. If your pattern is shorter than 35″, cut fewer strips.

Cut one 5″ strip and one 3″ strip from each of the five fabrics (total ten strips). This should give you approximately 35″ in length after the strips are flatlocked together. This allows 5″ for seam allowances.

For a Larger Piece of Flatlocked Fabric:

1 Use additional fabrics. You can use as many fabrics as you want. This is a good way to use up your leftover fabrics.

2 Cut the strips wider than specified above.

3 Make two pieces of flatlocked fabric.

Flatlocking the Strips Together

Serger Setup: Two- or Three-Thread Flatlock

Follow the recommended stitch settings in your manual to adjust your serger for a two- or three-thread flatlock stitch. Use the left needle and adjust to a wide stitch width. Start with a stitch length of 1 to 2 and adjust to your preference. The needle tension should be loose enough to allow the seam to open flat.

For a three-thread stitch, place the decorative thread in the upper looper. Use polyester thread in the needle and polyester or woolly nylon thread in the lower looper. For a two-thread stitch, place decorative in the lower looper and polyester thread in the needle. Test and adjust your stitches on two layers of fabric.

Serging

1 Arrange the strips in the desired sewing order, alternating the fabric widths. The most dominant strips will be those in the middle so place your favorite fabrics in the center area of the flatlocked fabric.

2 Using the flatlock stitch, serge the strips wrong-sides-together two at a time. Don't cut. Open the seams flat on each pair of strips before joining them to another set.

3 When all the strips are serged in pairs, serge the pairs together two at a time. This helps to minimize stretching and distortion. Always start serging from the same end each time so the direction of the stitching is consistent.

4 Continue serging all the sets together, two at a time. When you are finished serging all the strips together, only one selvage end will be even.

5 Using a press cloth, press all the seams flat from the wrong side of the fabric.

Optional Layout Variation

To lay out the strips to achieve a staggered or Bargello effect, sew this fabric in a circle (or tube shape). Remove the stitching at any seam within the strip so the fabric at the top of the strip will alternate.

1 Serge the last seam of the strips together to sew the fabric in a circle (or tube shape).

2 Lay the tube flat and square it up.

3 Cut six 1″-wide strips for the vest back. Set them aside.

4 Cut 2½″-wide strips through both layers of the remaining fabric.

5 Remove the flatlock stitching to take the seams apart where needed to achieve the desired layout.

6 Open and arrange the fabric strips in the correct order for serging.

7 Skip to "Arrange and Flatlock the Strips Together."

Cutting the Flatlocked Strips from Flat Fabric

1 Cut six 1″-wide strips for the vest back. Set them aside.

2 Cut 2½″-wide strips from the remaining fabric. You should have 14 or 15 strips, depending on the widths of fabrics used.

Arranging and Flatlocking the Strips Together

Lay the strips out by alternating the direction of every other one.

Continue using the same serger setup to flatlock the second strips together to create the finished fabric for the vest fronts.

SergeArt for the Vest Back
Serger Setup: Balanced Three-Thread Decorative Stitch

Use the same stitch width and length setting as for creating the flatlocked fabric. Set the serger for a balanced three-thread stitch. Use decorative thread in the upper looper, polyester in the needle and lower looper. Test your stitch settings and adjust by serging a leftover scrap of the flatlocked fabric.

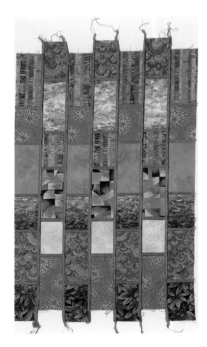

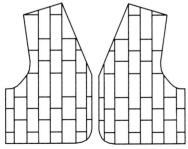

Serge around three sides on each of the strips cut earlier to use for the back. Don't cut the thread tails too short. Tuck them under before stitching them to the back.

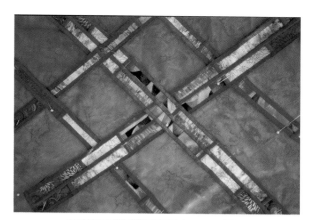

Putting It All Together

Cut out the vest fronts from the flatlocked fabric. Flip the pattern over to cut the second side.

Sewing Machine: Straight Stitch

1 Stitch the flatlocked vest front to the underlining fabric, 1/8″ from the outside edges. Treat both layers as one. The underlining reduces stress on the flatlocked seams.

2 To give the vest back more stability while stitching, iron a piece of Sulky Totally Stable Iron On Stabilizer to the wrong side of the fabric. Stitch through the stabilizer and tear it off when finished.

3 Arrange the strips on the vest back. Tuck the thread tails under the strips. Feel free to use your own designs for the placement. Pin, glue, or fuse the strips temporarily in place.

4 Stitch around the edges of all the strips. The sewing machine needle should come down into the stitching right next to the outer edge of the upper looper thread. Use Sulky invisible thread in the needle so the stitching line won't show. Use a decorative stitch presser foot with a groove in the bottom of the foot so it easily glides over the bulk of the serged edge.

Optional: Use a wide twin needle to stitch the strips.

Stitch strips on the back in the desired placement.

Vest Construction

Follow the instructions in Chapter 4 for final vest construction on the serger or use your favorite method.

Serger Setup: Balanced Four-Thread Construction Stitch

Set up your serger for a balanced four-thread construction stitch. Use polyester thread in the needles and loopers. Use a wide stitch width and a stitch length of 2½. Test your stitch settings and adjust by serging through four layers of fabric.

Variations

The following vests were made by flatlocking fabric together using different cutting methods for the fabrics.

The two odd-shaped pieces were made to be used as yokes on a jacket. You can use any leftover pieces of flatlocked fabric as yokes on other garments.

The fabrics you use for flatlocking can be cut into any width, size, or shape. The choice is yours.

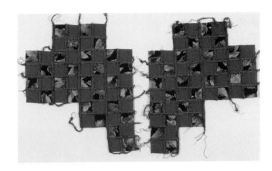

Flatlocked fabric for yokes.

The flatlocked patchwork vest with a Mardi Gras theme was made by Connie Hoke, Houston.

Another flatlocked patchwork vest with a Mardi Gras theme made by Connie Hoke.

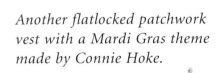

CHAPTER 11

Ultra Crazy Vest

Materials

- Panel Vest pattern by Judy Bishop Designs (or favorite vest pattern)
- Ultrasuede scraps or squares - measure pattern pieces and buy enough Ultrasuede to cover front panels and back
- Ultrasuede or lining fabric for side vest panels - cut the pattern on the crossgrain and it usually takes no more than 1/3 yard
- lining fabric - follow pattern recommendations
- underlining - only for side panels
- fusible knit interfacing - enough for front panels and partial back
- freezer paper (enough to make two complete copies of both front panels and partial back)
- several spools decorative serger thread that fit through eye of needle (rayon, woolly nylon, metallic, etc.)
- 2 cones matching polyester thread for loopers
- size 80/12 embroidery or topstitching needle (with a large eye)
- extra fine point Sharpie marker

The Ultra Crazypatch Vest was designed to use up some of the Ultrasuede scraps in my stash and was made using the Panel Vest pattern by Judy Bishop Designs. I've been collecting Ultrasuede for years in every possible color. This garment gave me the perfect excuse to fondle my collection and use some of the beautiful colors in a project. The crazypatch fabric was made from scraps and the side panels and front band were cut from larger pieces. I joined the strips of Ultrasuede together with a flatlock stitch to get the right length for the front band.

Other types of fabric can be used for this technique, but it's best to use fabrics that don't ravel easily. Knits will work if they are backed with a soft interfacing to keep them from stretching. This method of making crazypatch fabric will work to create yardage of any size.

TIP

If the Ultrasuede scraps need to be prewashed, put them in a pillowcase, tie the end, then wash and dry. Some colors may bleed. Check for colorfastness before mixing colors.

Making the Pattern for Crazypatch Fabric

Make freezer paper patterns of the areas to be patchworked. You will need two left front panels, two right front panels, and two partial backs. Trace just the outline of the pattern pieces to be used for patchwork fabric on freezer paper. Make two copies of each pattern piece. Use one set of freezer paper patterns to make the iron-on patterns used to cut the Ultrasuede. The other set is the master pattern for placement.

> ## TIP
>
> *When cutting multiple patterns, this method is faster than cutting each pattern piece individually. Tear off a piece of freezer paper large enough to cut two copies of the pattern piece and fold it in half. Place the folded paper on a cutting mat and lay the pattern on top of the paper as if cutting fabric. Cut the pattern out with a rotary cutter through both layers of freezer paper at the same time.*

Ultra crazypatch fabric

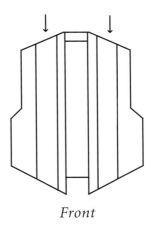

Front

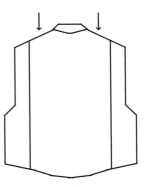

Back
*Separate center panels
and side panels*

Front panel

Back panel

Draw the Crazypatch Design on the Paper Pattern

It is very important to make a master pattern and a duplicate pattern to cut apart. Without a master pattern, it will be like trying to put together a jigsaw puzzle without the picture on the box to guide you. You will not regret taking the time for the next steps.

Front panels

Stitching order for crazypatch fabric. The arrows designate corners. Front (LF) (RF)

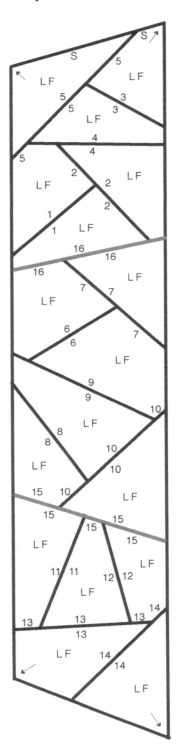
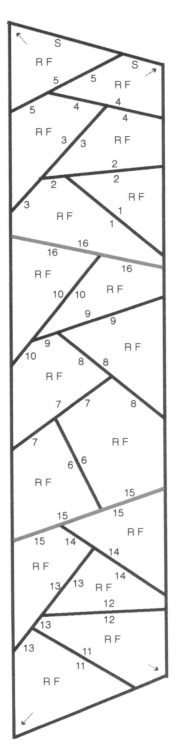

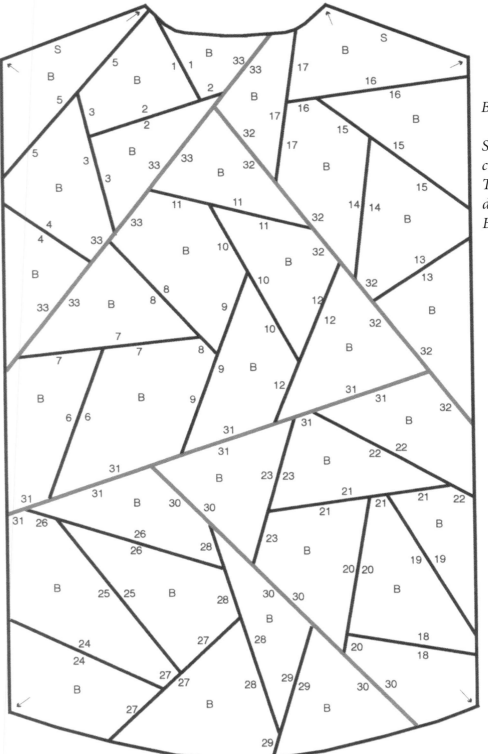

Back panel

Stitching order for crazypatch fabric. The arrows designate corners. Back (B)

The patterns in the illustrations have been reversed so the lapels will be on the correct side when finished. The right side of the finished fabric will not be a mirror image.

The instructions are for making a vest using the Panel Vest pattern, but the same method is used for any pattern. You can make the sections larger if desired.

1 On one set of freezer paper patterns for the left and a right front panel, use an extra fine point marker and ruler to divide both of the freezer paper patterns into three large sections.

2 Divide each of these sections in five smaller sections.

3 Look at each of the three large sections and decide the sewing order for the smaller sections. The sewing order usually corresponds to the drawing order. Number the sewing order of the patches in each section. (The sewing order is shown in the illustration for the Panel Vest. Use it as reference if using another pattern.)

4 Mark each of the patches with LF for left front and RF for right front.

5 Divide one copy of the back into five large sections.

6 Divide each of the large sections into smaller sections.

7 Number the sewing order of the patches in each section.

8 Mark each of the patches with B for the back.

9 Decide on the color placement and write it on each section of the patterns.

10 Lay the second set of patterns on top of the marked set to make duplicate patterns. Trace the cutting lines and numbers for the sewing order. The duplicates are used as master patterns and don't need the RF, LF, and B and fabric colors written on them. Those markings are only necessary on the set that will be cut apart.

Cutting Ultrasuede Pieces for Crazypatch Fabric

1 Cut apart the patterns for the Ultrasuede. Leave the master pattern intact.

2 Separate the pieces by color.

3 Place the pattern pieces on the Ultrasuede with the shiny side to the wrong side of the fabric. Leave enough room between the pattern pieces to add 1/8″ seam allowances on each side.

4 Use medium heat and iron the pattern pieces to the back of the Ultrasuede.

5 Add 1/8″ seam allowances around all sides of each pattern piece and cut the Ultrasuede pieces for the patchwork.

6 Place the cut out sections on the master pattern, matching the numbers for the sewing order.

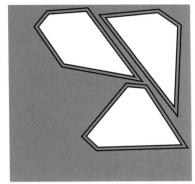

Iron the pattern to the wrong side of the fabric. The inside line is the edge of the pattern. The outside line is the cutting line with 1/8″ seam allowance added.

Serger Setup: Two- or Three-Thread Flatlock

Set your serger for a two- or three-thread flatlock stitch. Use a wide stitch width and a stitch length between 1 and 2. For a three-thread stitch, thread the upper and lower looper with polyester serger thread and decorative thread in the needle. For a two-thread stitch, use polyester in the lower looper and decorative thread in the needle. Test and adjust your stitches on two layers of fabric.

Serging the Crazypatch Fabric

Don't trim the edges of the Ultrasuede pieces as you serge them. Any trimming will affect the finished size of the crazypatch fabric. Only the points that stick out will need to be trimmed off.

Try not to stretch the Ultrasuede while serging or you'll end up with distortion in the finished crazypatch fabric. If the fabric stretches, set the differential feed toward 2 to slightly ease the fabric. Test on a scrap of the fabric to adjust for the correct setting.

The freezer paper patterns can be ironed on fabric several times. Keep them sorted in separate stacks when removing them from the fabric.

1 Serge all the pieces right-sides-together for one large section at a time. Follow the sewing order in the illustrations.

2 Match the numbers for the sewing order. Line up the edges

to be serged with right-sides-together. The points of one piece need to extend past the edges of the other one, the width of the seam allowance.

③ Peel off the paper and serge the seam.

④ Open each flatlocked seam before adding another piece.

⑤ Lay the serged sections in place on the master to pick up the next piece to add.

⑥ When a section is finished, place it on the master pattern.

⑦ When all the large sections are finished, serge them together to finish the fabric.

> ### TIP
>
> *Place the fabric patch with the most seams on top and the patch with fewer seams toward the feed dogs. This allows the fabric to feed through the serger much more easily and also minimizes shifting.*

Putting It All Together

Cutting

① Cut the vest lining.

② Cut underlining for the side panels to balance the weight of the Ultrasuede sections.

③ Cut knit interfacing for the partial back and front panels. Fuse it to the back of the crazypatch fabric. This will take the stress off the flatlocked seams.

Final Vest Construction

Follow the instructions for construction that are included with the Panel Vest pattern to finish with a front band. They are written for the sewing machine. This method of construction is well suited for this style of vest. Serge finish all raw edges before sewing the seams on the sewing machine. Use 1/2″ seam allowances for constructing the Panel Vest.

Note: If using a different pattern, follow those instructions for completing the garment.

Ultra crazypatch vest and skirt made by Connie Hoke, Houston.

CHAPTER 12
Flatlocked
Lapel Coat

Materials

- Lapel Coat pattern by Judy Bishop Designs (or similar pattern)
- coat fabric - follow pattern recommendations
- lining fabric - follow pattern recommendations
- underlining fabric - follow pattern recommendations
- interfacing - follow pattern recommendations
- 1/4 yd each of 4 different cotton fabrics to use for patchwork yokes (1/3 yd of fabric #4 for size XL and XXL)

- 2 spools decorative serger thread to coordinate with fabrics (rayon, woolly nylon, metallic, etc.)
- 2 cones matching polyester thread for needle and lower looper
- Sulky invisible thread
- 2 yds 1/8″ piping or piping cord (Make your own piping on the serger by covering this cord with matching fabric using a piping foot, or use ready-made piping.)
- piping foot for the serger or sewing machine

This garment is my serged interpretation of the sketch included with the Lapel Coat pattern by Judy Bishop Designs. The pattern can be made as a coat or vest. I made the vest version because it is way too hot in Texas to wear long sleeves very often.

The collar was stitched with a two-thread chain stitch available only on five-thread sergers. If you don't have that option on your serger, make serger chain braid and stitch it to the collar or design your own embellishment.

Illustration from the Lapel Coat pattern by Judy Bishop Designs.

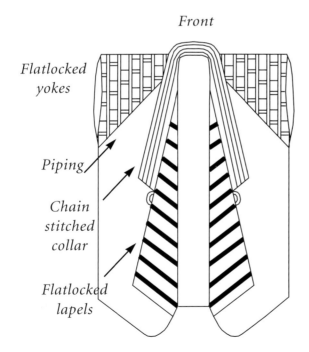

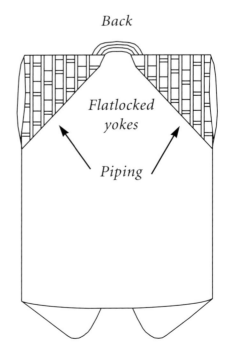

Front

Back

Flatlocked yokes

Piping

Chain stitched collar

Flatlocked lapels

Flatlocked yokes

Piping

Cutting the Coat

1 Trace or cut the pattern in your size.

2 Follow the pattern instructions and cut out all the pieces for the coat. Cut the lapels at least 2″ larger than the pattern all the way around. They will be recut later, after flatlocking.

3 Follow the pattern instructions to cut the lining and underlining.

Measuring the Pattern

The cutting instructions are provided for making flatlocked fabric for the yokes of the Lapel Coat pattern in all sizes. The first measurements given are for extra small to large. For sizes XL and XXL, see the measurements listed in parentheses.

If using a different pattern, measure the pattern to determine what size to make the finished fabric. Cut enough strips to make two mirror image pieces of flatlocked fabric the length and width needed. There are four yokes (left front and back, and right front and back).

Cutting Fabric for Flatlocked Yokes

The finished size of each piece of the flatlocked fabric is approximately 15″ x 17″.

Fabric #1 - cut 3 strips 1″ x 18″
Fabric #2 - cut 3 strips 2″ x 18″
Fabric #3 - cut 3 strips 3″ x 18″
Fabric #4 - cut 6 strips 1¼″ x 18″, cut 4 strips 2″ x 18″
(For size XL or XXL, cut 8 strips 1¼″ x 18″ and 4 strips 2″ x 18″ of Fabric #4.)

Flatlocking the Patchwork Fabric

Serger Setup: Two- or Three-Thread Flatlock

Follow the recommended stitch settings in your manual to adjust your serger for a two- or three-thread flatlock stitch. Use the left needle and adjust to a wide stitch width. Start with a stitch length of 1 to 2 and adjust to your preference. The needle tension should be loose enough to allow the seam to open flat.

For a three-thread stitch, place the decorative thread in the upper looper. Use polyester thread in the needle and polyester or woolly nylon thread in the lower looper. For a two-thread stitch, place decorative in the lower looper and polyester thread in the needle. Test and adjust your stitches on two layers of fabric.

Serging the First Set of Strips

① Serge the strips from Fabric #2, #3, and #4 together, following the suggested layout. Open the seams each time before adding a new strip.

② Press the flat fabric on the wrong side.

③ Serge the last seam of the strips together to sew it in a circle (or tube shape).

④ Lay the tube flat and square it up.

⑤ Cut 1¾″ strips through both layers of fabric for a total of eight strips. (If making size XL or XXL, cut ten strips.)

Place the strips in this order

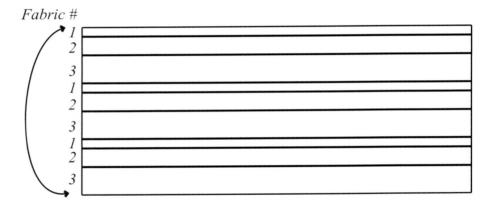

Connect these two edges to form a tube

Flatlocking All the Strips Together

Make two pieces of fabric that are mirror images. The pattern of the fabric strips on the left of the diagram stagger upward from left to right. The pattern of the fabric strips in the right diagram stagger upward from right to left.

① Remove the flatlock stitching to take the seams apart where needed, to open and arrange the fabric strips in the order on the diagram.

② Trim the strips from Fabric #4 to exactly the same length as the flatlocked strips.

③ Flatlock the pieced strips to the solid strips wrong-sides-together. Open each seam flat before adding another strip.

④ Use a press cloth and press the fabric from the wrong side. You are now ready to cut the front and back yokes from the flatlocked fabric.

Arrange the strips in this order

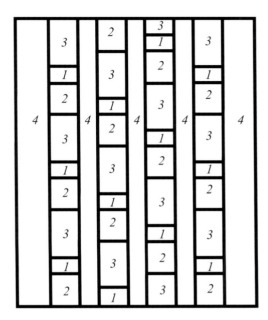

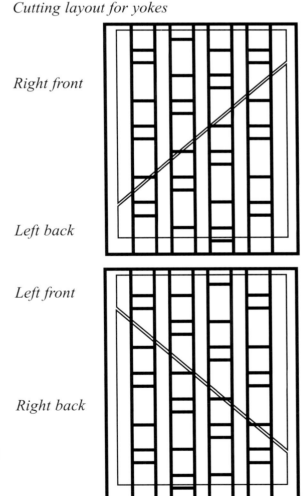

Cutting layout for yokes

Right front

Left back

Left front

Right back

Cutting the Yokes

1 Cut the yokes, following the layout in the diagram. Don't forget to flip the pattern over to cut the other side so you will have both a left and right side. It is better to trace two patterns of the yoke.

2 Mark one of the patterns with left front on one side and right back on the other. Mark the second one with right front on one side and left back on the other. This helps reduce confusion.

Marking the Lapels

1 Place one lapel on top of the other right-sides-together. Make sure the edges are even all the way around. This step is important to ensure that the stitching lines are evenly spaced on each side of the coat.

2 Start measuring from the bottom of the lapel along the diagonal straight edge that comes up from the curve. Add 2″ to the first interval only, to allow for the excess fabric that was added when the pattern was cut. The finished Lapel Coat in the photo was flatlocked at 1½″ intervals, but the snips can

Lapel
The fabric is cut 2" larger than the pattern. The inner line is the pattern, the outer line is the cut edge of the fabric.

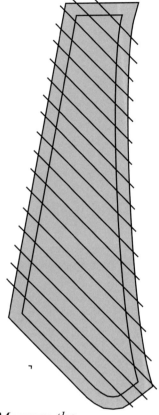

Measure the first line from this edge. Add 2" to the first interval to make the first snips. Make snips in the fabric only at the outer edge of each side. Fold the fabric across the snips to serge.

be made at any interval you choose.

❸ Make short snips through both layers of fabric along both sides of the lapels at equal intervals.

Flatlocking the Lapels

Continue with the same serger setup as used on the flatlocked fabric for the yokes. Test serge on a scrap of the coat fabric to adjust the stitch settings.

Practice on a scrap of the coat fabric to see how much fabric to let hang off the edge of the fabric so the stitch will open up totally flat instead of having a little fold of fabric inside the stitching. Use a seam guide if one is available for your serger. You can also use a blind hem foot if it can be used with the left needle position.

❶ Fold the lapel fabric diagonally from snip to snip.

❷ Serge along the fold, letting the thread hang off the edge of the fabric.

❸ Open the stitches flat each time you serge a row.

❹ Serge all the lines, folding the fabric at the snips on both lapels. Start each new row of stitching on the same side of the fabric.

❺ Press from the wrong side. Iron lightweight interfacing to the wrong side of the fabric, covering the back side of the flatlock stitching.

❻ Lay the lapel pattern piece on the flatlocked lapel fabric and cut it out one at a time so you can line up the stitching and cut the sides to match.

Collar

The collar can be embellished with serger chain braid or a two-thread chain stitch (on a five-thread serger only). Use the embellishment of choice.

1 Iron lightweight interfacing to the back of both sides of the collar fabric.

2 Mark placement lines on the wrong side of the fabric for the chain stitch. Mark on the right side to attach serger chain braid.

Serger Setup: Two-Thread Chain Stitch

Refer to your manual to adjust the serger for a two-thread chain stitch. Use a thick decorative thread in the chain stitch looper and polyester thread in the needle.

Serge along the marked lines with the fabric wrong-side-up.

Two-thread chain stitch with 30 wt. rayon thread in the looper.

Making Fabric-Covered Piping

You can make fabric-covered piping on the serger or sewing machine or use ready-made piping. If making it with your serger, you'll need a piping foot and if making it on your sewing machine, you'll need a piping or zipper foot.

Serger Setup: Balanced Three- or Four-Thread Construction Stitch

Put the piping foot on the serger. Set it to a wide stitch width and stitch length of 2½. Use polyester thread in the needles and loopers. For a three-thread stitch, use the left needle.

Serging

1 Cut strips 1½″-wide by the length needed for the lower edges of the yokes.

2 Fold the fabric around the filler cord, leaving about 2″ extending past the ends of the fabric.

3 Raise the foot and place the fabric and cord under it with the filler cord in the piping groove under the foot. Make sure the cord stays in the groove while serging.

4 Serge the raw edge of the fabric, cutting away excess fabric.

Putting It All Together

Attaching the Yokes

Use any method you prefer to attach the piping to the yokes (sewing machine or serger). If you attach the piping with the sewing machine, grade the seam allowances before sewing the yokes to the coat.

1 Serge or sew the piping to the lower edge of the yoke pieces.

2 Fold the piping seam allowances to the wrong side and press.

3 Place the yokes on the coat front and back. Line up the flatlock seams of the yokes to match at the shoulder seams. Pin the yokes in place on the coat.

4 Straight stitch the yokes in place right in the seamline between the edge of the yoke and the piping. The yoke shoulder seams are treated as one layer with the coat fabric.

Final Garment Construction

Follow the instructions included with the pattern to finish the garment construction. The Lapel Coat pattern is best suited to construction on the sewing machine. Serge the underlining to the coat fabric. Use 1/2″ seam allowances for constructing the Lapel Coat.

CHAPTER 13

Seminole Twist Vest

Materials

- Panel Vest pattern by Judy Bishop Designs
- 3 different cotton fabrics for vest (more for sizes XL and up)
  - 1¼ yd Fabric #1 main print - side panels, strips
  - 1¼ yd Fabric #2 coordinate - front panel, strips
  - 1/2 yd Fabric #3 coordinate - strips, front band
- lining fabric - follow pattern recommendations
- underlining - same yardage as lining
- spool Sulky invisible thread or thread to match Fabric #2 (for use in the sewing machine)
- 2 different colors woolly nylon decorative serger thread to coordinate with fabrics
- cone polyester thread for needle
- 4 cones matching polyester thread for construction

The embellishments on the Panel Vest pattern by Judy Bishop Designs are serged with a balanced three-thread decorative stitch using a different color thread in each looper. This is a very decorative stitch when using two different thread colors.

I created Seminole patchwork fabric with a "twist" for the back of the vest. The direction of the serged seams alternate to make the twisted effect. The front panel features twisted tucks that add another twist to this vest. The tucks are serged and then straight stitched on the sewing machine in alternate directions to get the twisted effect. (If you're not twisted before using these techniques, you certainly will be afterward.)

Choose a small to medium size print fabric to start with. Don't choose an overly large print because the design will get lost when the fabric is cut into 2″-wide strips. Select two coordinating fabrics that will blend with the main fabric, but not compete for attention.

Because you can use many different fabrics, Seminole patchwork is a great way to use up leftover fabric from other projects. The largest pieces of fabric needed are for the front tucks and side panels.

Front and back side panels

Twisted tucks

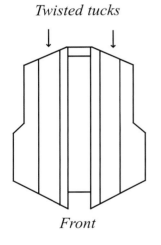

Front

Seminole twist patchwork

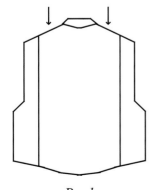

Back
Separate center panel and side panels

Measuring the Pattern to Make Seminole Twist Fabric

If using a different pattern, measure the pattern pieces to determine what size to make the embellished fabrics. To economize on decorative thread, make the Seminole twist fabric close to the exact size you need. Refer to Chapter 1 for information on measuring your pattern to determine yardage.

Making the Seminole Twist Fabric

Cutting

The measurements given here are for the partial back pattern of the Panel Vest. Cut strips from each of the three fabrics the width given below for your size. Cut the strips across the fabric from selvage to selvage.

Fabric #1 - cut 6 strips 2″-wide for size small/medium, 2¼″-wide for size large, and 2½″-wide for size XL

Fabric #2 - cut 3 strips 2″-wide for size small/medium, 2¼″-wide for size large, and 2½″-wide for size XL

Fabric #3 - cut 3 strips 2″-wide for size small/medium, 2¼″-wide for size large, and 2½″-wide for size XL

To make a larger piece of Seminole twist fabric than the size needed for the partial back pattern, you can either use more than three fabrics (as many as you want), cut the strips wider than specified, or cut more strips.

Arranging the Strips

❶ With the strips laid out in the order shown in the diagram, Fabric #1 will always be the strip placed on top when serging the strips together.

❷ Place all print fabrics with the design pointing in the same direction.

Serge the strips in the following order

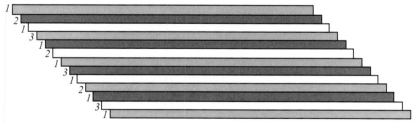

Offset the selvage ends by 1½″ when adding each strip

Serging the Strips

Serger Setup: Wide Three-Thread Balanced Decorative Stitch

❶ Thread your serger with a different color decorative thread in each looper. Use polyester cone thread in the left needle.

❷ Follow the recommended stitch settings (tension adjustments) in your manual for a wide three-thread balanced stitch. The looper tensions are set at a balanced, normal setting.

Adjust for the type of thread you are using. The looper threads should meet exactly at the cut edge of the fabric.

❸ Start with a stitch length of 1 to 1½ and adjust until satisfied with the texture and amount of thread coverage. Test your stitch settings and adjust by serging two layers of fabric.

Serging the First Set of Strips

Always start serging from the same end of the strips each time so the direction of the stitching is consistent. Each color thread should face the same direction when the fabric is completed.

Serge the strips (and sets) together two at a time to minimize stretching and distortion. Keep the strips in order by leaving them chained together. Cut them from the chain when needed.

Serge all the strips wrong-sides-together. Offset each strip and each set of strips by 1½″ before serging. By offsetting the strips, you will have more usable fabric when you need to cut it again at a 45° angle (see diagram).

Don't trim any fabric off the edges of the strips as you serge them. Keep the width of the strips exactly the size they are cut. The pieced fabric will warp out of shape if the strips are uneven.

❶ Pick up the first two strips and place them wrong-sides-together. Line up the selvage edge of the top strip 1½″ down from the selvage edge of the bottom strip. The bottom strip will always stick out farther than the top strip.

❷ Serge the strips together two at a time until they are all in sets of two.

❸ Offset the sets of strips by 1½″ before serging them together. Serge two sets together at a time.

❹ Continue serging all the sets together until all sets are joined. When finished serging the strips together, both selvage ends should be staggered.

❺ Using a press cloth on the right side, press all the seams in the same direction.

Cutting & Serging the Fabric Again to Make the Final Seminole Twist Fabric

Use a ruler with markings for a 45° angle. Cut the serged fabric into strips the same width the first strips were cut (based on your size) at a 45° angle.

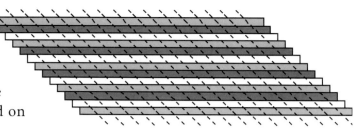

Cut the serged fabric into strips again at a 45° angle

Making Seminole twist patchwork fabric

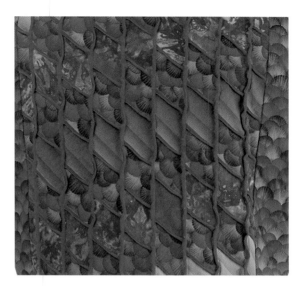

Close-up of the vest back.

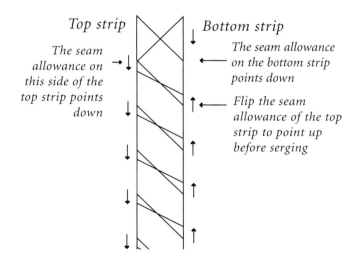

Top strip   Bottom strip

The seam allowance on this side of the top strip points down

The seam allowance on the bottom strip points down

Flip the seam allowance of the top strip to point up before serging

Serging

Continue to serge the strips and the sets together two at a time to minimize stretching and distortion since the strips are now cut on the bias. Set the differential feed toward 2 to further prevent the seams from stretching. Adjust for the correct setting on a scrap of the strips.

❶ Place the strips wrong-sides-together with the decorative seam allowances pointing down.

❷ As you serge these strips together, flip up each seam allowance of the top layer as you come to it to alternate the direction of the seams. This is what gives the twist to the Seminole fabric. Continue until all sets are joined.

❸ The sides of the finished fabric will now be at an angle. One more seam is all it takes to complete the Seminole twist fabric and square it up for cutting the pattern.

❹ Lay the fabric on a cutting mat or table with the jagged edges at the top, even on a straight edge.

5 Between the first and second strip on the left, cut one side of the fabric off at a square angle to the jagged edge. This will leave the entire length of one strip on the edge that needs to be serged to the other side.

6 Move that section to the other side of the Seminole fabric and line it up so the design matches. Serge the section to the other side. The Seminole twist fabric is now squared up and ready to use.

7 Cut the partial back pattern from your new fabric.

Line up the top edge of the fabric along a straight edge.

Cut off this section of the fabric between the first and second strip, leaving one whole strip intact along the edge.

Serge the cut section to this side to square up the fabric.

Cutting line

The twisted seams have been left out of this diagram so the cutting line can be seen.

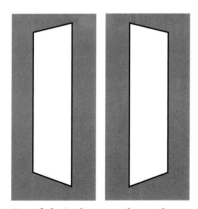

Cut fabric larger than the pattern to allow for tucks.

Cutting Fabric for the Twisted Tucks Front Panels

Cut two oversized pieces of Fabric #2 to make the tucked fabric for the front panels. Each tuck uses 1/2″ of fabric. Multiply the total number of tucks you are making by 1/2″ (or .5). Add this total to the width of the front panel pattern and add a few inches to this total.

1 Measure the width and length of the front panel pattern. Add 5″ to the width and 3″ to the length. Cut two pieces of fabric this size.

2 Mark four lengthwise lines 1¼″ apart, centered on the front panel fabric.

3 Press a fold along each of the marked lines.

Serging the Twisted Tucks

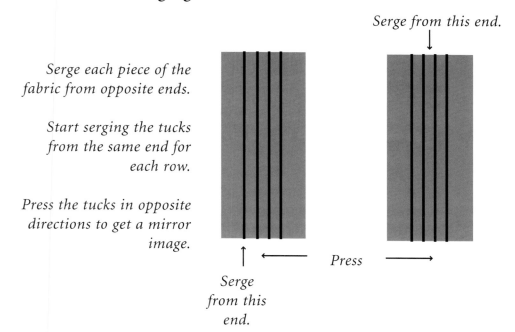

Serge from this end.

Serge each piece of the fabric from opposite ends.

Start serging the tucks from the same end for each row.

Press the tucks in opposite directions to get a mirror image.

Press

Serge from this end.

Serger Setup: Same Settings as for Seminole Twist Fabric

❶ Serge the tucks along the folds. Guide the fabric evenly and don't cut the folded edge. Start serging each piece of fabric from the same end each time, so the direction of the stitching is consistent and the same color thread stays on the same side of the tuck.

❷ Serge the tucks on the second piece from the opposite end of the fabric to make them mirror images. Maintain an even speed so the stitch quality stays consistent.

❸ Lay the tucked fabric so the same color thread is toward the middle.

❹ Use a press cloth to press the tucks in opposite directions.

Variations

Mark stitching lines every 2˝

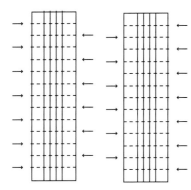

Alternate the direction of the stitching.
Begin the first row of straight stitching in opposite directions so you will have a right and left panel. Be sure to flip the pattern over when cutting out the panels from the finished fabric.

Make straight or twisted tucks over ribbon, yarn, cording, etc. with three threads, using Sulky invisible thread in the upper looper and a decorative thread in the lower looper.

Sewing Machine: Straight Stitch

By straight stitching the tucks in alternate directions you get a wavy effect with the two colors of looper thread.

❶ Mark stitching lines every 2˝ on the fabric across the tucks. You lose the wave effect if you space the stitching lines too far apart. Mark the lines 1½˝ apart for sizes small and medium.
❷ Set up your sewing machine for a straight stitch. Use a stitch length of 2.5 (or 10 to 12 stitches per inch). Use Sulky invisible thread for the top and polyester thread to match the fabric in the bobbin. Reduce the upper tension if the stitching puckers the fabric.
❸ Straight stitch across the tucks along each marked line. Stitch the top row of each panel in opposite directions so the panels will be mirror images of each other. Stitch each row in alternating directions.

Putting It All Together

Cutting

❶ Center the pattern over the tucked fabric. Cut out a left and right front panel. Be sure to flip the pattern over.
❷ Cut the partial back pattern from the Seminole twist fabric.
❸ Cut the front and back side panels for the outer vest from Fabric #1.

4 Cut the front band from Fabric #3

5 Cut lining for the vest front panel, front and back side panels, and the partial back.

6 Cut out all vest sections for the underlining.

Final Garment Construction

You can construct the vest on the serger or the sewing machine. I prefer the bias binding method due to the bulk of all the decorative seam allowances. Use whatever method you prefer.

Sewing Machine

Follow the instructions that are included with the pattern for final construction. They are written for the sewing machine.

For Serged Construction & Bias Edge Finish
Serger Setup: Balanced Four-Thread Construction Stitch

Set up your serger for a balanced four-thread construction stitch. Use polyester thread in the needles and loopers. Use a wide stitch width and a stitch length of 2½. Test your stitch settings and adjust by serging through four layers of fabric.

1 Serge the front and back side panels together at the shoulder seam.

2 Serge the front panels and the partial back together at the shoulder seams.

3 Serge the side panel section to the front panel/back section, matching seamlines at the shoulders.

4 Serge the side seams.

5 Repeat steps 1-4 to construct the lining.

6 Place the vest lining inside the outer vest wrong-sides-together. Line up all the edges and seamlines. Trim the layers to match if needed.

7 Cut 3″-wide bias strips. Join the strips with a straight stitch to make a length of bias to go around all the raw edges of the vest and the armholes. Fold and press the strip in half lengthwise.

8 Stitch the bias strip on all the unfinished edges with a straight stitch or serge it on. Turn the bias strip to the wrong side and stitch in the ditch from the right side to catch the folded edge of the bias on the back.

9 Press the garment using a press cloth.

CHAPTER 14
Shirred Vest

Materials

- favorite vest pattern (suggested yardage works for vests up to 24″ long)
- 2/3 yd main fabric
- 1/2 yd coordinating fabric for shirring
- yardage of either of the two above fabrics the vest back length
- lining fabric - follow pattern recommendations
- 4 cones matching polyester serger thread
- shirring/gathering foot for serger

The fabric for this vest is created with the shirring foot, my favorite accessory foot for the serger. This foot works by using the differential feed feature (if you don't have differential feed, the foot won't work). You can gather one layer of fabric and attach it to a flat layer all in one step.

The entire vest front pattern is cut from the finished fabric. Another option is to cut the pattern into sections, placing the sections at different angles to cut them out, then putting them back together to complete the fabric. The back of the vest is not embellished, but you can consider this a blank canvas to add embellishments of your choice.

It's important to experiment with this foot before starting your project. Practice shirring with scraps of the same fabric you will be using for the garment.

When Shirring Fabric:

❶ Choose fabrics of similar weight.

❷ Prewash to remove sizing that may stiffen the fabric.

❸ Avoid using stiff or heavyweight fabrics - they don't gather well.

Fabric Selection

Use small prints for the fabric that will be gathered and larger prints for the flat sections.

Don't use fabrics with a definite print that should match from top to bottom. The flat strips may shift while being serged and the design will not match.

Cutting Strips for Shirred Fabric

These measurements will make two pieces of shirred fabric approximately 20″ x 26″. Cut out all the strips needed to create the shirred fabric. If you need to make the fabric larger, cut the strips wider or add more strips.

❶ From the main fabric, cut four 5½″ x 44″ strips. Cut the 44″

length in half for a total of eight 5½"-wide strips. Keep them in order if using a print fabric.

❷ From the coordinating fabric, cut six 2½" x 44" strips for shirring. Do *not* cut these strips in half. The strips to be gathered need to be twice as long as the strip that stays flat.

Creating the Fabric

Serger Setup: Balanced Four-Thread Construction Stitch

❶ Put the shirring foot on the serger. Set the differential feed at 2 for the maximum amount of gathering.

❷ Set up the serger for a balanced four-thread construction stitch. Use polyester thread in the needles and loopers. Use a wide stitch width and a stitch length of 2½. Test your stitch settings and adjust by serging through two layers of fabric.

TIP

To increase gathering, increase the differential feed setting and/or increase the stitch length.

Shirring

Make two pieces of shirred fabric. There are four 5½" strips and three 2½" strips in each finished piece of fabric.

❶ Place the 2½"-wide strip of fabric to be gathered under the separator blade of the shirring foot, with the end of the strip right under the needle.

❷ Place the 5½" strip of fabric that stays flat in the slot of the foot.

❸ Line up the ends of both strips at the needle.

❹ Turn the flywheel by hand and bring the needle down into both layers of fabric. This anchors the fabric for you to get your hands in position and allows the fabrics to start gathering evenly.

❺ When guiding the layers, let the bottom layer of fabric slip lightly through your fingers as you slowly serge the layers together. Don't put any tension on the bottom layer or the gathers won't be as full. Keep the fabrics aligned at the edges without cutting.

❻ Trim away any excess fabric from the narrow strip that didn't gather. Start serging from the trimmed end to attach the next flat strip.

❼ Place the trimmed end of the gathered strip under the separator blade all the way to the needle and attach it to another flat strip, following the previous instructions. It's

The fabric for shirring is on the bottom. The fabric that stays flat is on the top.

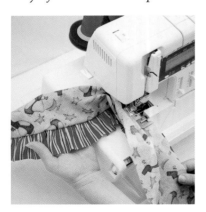

The amount of gathering is controlled by the differential feed setting.

important to serge slowly and not hold back the bottom layer of fabric.

8 Continue until you have completed both pieces of fabric

Cutting

1 Place the vest front pattern on the shirred fabric at a diagonal angle. Don't place points or corners on the shirred strips or it will be hard to line up all the gathers when serging the garment together.

2 Cut out the vest front.

3 Turn the pattern over and place it on the second piece of fabric with the diagonal angle in the opposite direction.

4 Cut the second side of the vest front.

5 Follow pattern recommendations to cut the lining.

6 Cut the vest back from the fabric of choice.

Final Garment Construction

Follow the instructions in Chapter 4 for final vest construction on the serger or use your favorite method.

Serge the vest with the lining fabric toward the feed dogs and the shirred fabric on top. This will help keep the gathers evenly distributed and caught in the seam.

Serger Setup: Balanced Four-Thread Construction Stitch

Set up your serger for a balanced four-thread construction stitch. Use polyester thread in the needles and loopers. Use a wide stitch width and a stitch length of 2½. Test your stitch settings and adjust by serging through four layers of fabric.

One strip shirred to flat fabric.

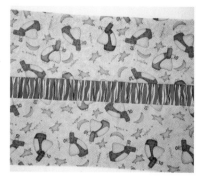

Shirred strip inserted between flat fabric.

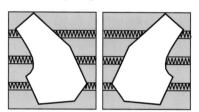

Diagonal layout on the shirred fabric

TIP

If the shirred sections spread open too far at the cut edges when constructing the garment, fuse narrow strips of iron-on stabilizer to the wrong side of the gathers. Serge as usual, then remove the stabilizer.

Variation: Jigsaw Vest

❶ Make a copy of the pattern and divide it into several large sections. Add 1/2″ seam allowances to each section or add them to each seamline when cutting the fabric apart.

❷ Place the pattern sections at different angles on the shirred fabric to cut them out. Don't place the corners on the shirred strips.

❸ Trim away a scant 1/4″ when serging the sections back together.

❹ Place the original pattern on top of the fabric and trim to size.

The shirred fabric can be put back together with or without piping between the pieces. You can use ready-made piping or make some on the serger. Follow the instructions for the Flatlocked Lapel Coat to make piping on the serger.

Jigsaw vest. The shirred fabric was cut into sections and serged back together with piping insertion.

Finished fabric for vest fronts.

Resources

FABRICS

A & J Sewing Depot
10076 Kleckley
Houston, TX 77075

Collins Creations
(Ultrasuede)
(800) 374-4078

fabrics etcetera
571 W. Bay Area Blvd.
Webster, TX 77598

Lee Anne's Batiks
2605 Oceanfront Walk
San Diego, CA 92109

PATTERNS

Judy Bishop Designs
Dept. D
24603 Island Ave.
Carson, CA 90745

Park Bench Pattern Co.
P.O. Box 1089
Petaluma, CA 94953-1089
(707) 781-9142

Patterns by Carol McKinney
McKinney Enterprises, Inc.
1506 Allendale
Pasadena, TX 77502

NOTIONS & THREAD

American & Efird, Inc.
400 E. Central Ave.
Mt. Holly, NC 28120

DARR, Inc.
2370-G Hillcrest Rd. #121
Mobile, AL 36695

Dream World Enterprises, Inc.
P.O. Box 192
Bonners Ferry, ID 83805

Omnigrid
P.O. Box 663
Burlington, WA 98233

Robison-Anton Textile Co.
P.O. Box 159
Fairview, NJ 07022

SEW-ERGO
333 Wisteria Way
Lafayette, CO 80026

Sulky of America
3113 Broadpoint Dr.
Harbor Heights, FL 33983

ThreadPRO
(214) 369-1614
Fax (214) 369-4449
Email
thredpro@airmail.net

YLI Corp.
161 W. Main Street
Rock Hill, SC 29730

SERGERS

Tacony - Babylock
1760 Gilsinn Left Needle
Fenton, MO 63026

Elna USA
1760 Gilsinn Ln.
Fenton, MO 63026

Husqvarna/Viking
VWS, Inc.
11760 Berea Rd.
Cleveland, OH 44111

Janome/New Home
100 Hollister Rd.
Teterboro, NJ 07608

Juki Union Special
5 Haul Rd.
700 E. State St.
Wayne, NJ 07470

Pfaff American Sales Corp.
610 Winters Ave.
Paramus, NJ 07653

Bibliography

Serging

Baker, Naomi, and Gail Brown and Cindy Kacynski. *The Ultimate Serger Answer Guide*. Iola, WI: Krause Publications, 1996

Benton, Kitty. *Easy Guide to Serging Fine Fabrics*. Newtown, CT: The Taunton Press, Inc., 1997.

Boyce, Ann. *A New Serge in Wearable Art*, Iola, WI: Krause Publications., 1995.

Dodson, Jackie, and Jan Saunders. *Sew & Serge Terrific Textures*. Iola, WI: Krause Publications, 1996.

Drexler, Joyce. *Updated Serger Concepts in Sulky*, Sulky of America, Harbor Heights, Florida, 1991.

Dunn, April. *Deco Serging*. Columbus, OH: Dragon Threads, 1997.

Palmer, Pati, Gail Brown, and Sue Green. *The New Creative Serging Illustrated: The Complete Guide to Decorative Overlock Sewing*. 2nd ed. Iola, WI: Krause Publications, 1994.

Saunders, Jan. *Sew, Serge, Press: Speed Tailoring In the Ultimate Sewing Center*, Iola, WI: Krause Publications, 1989.

PBS Broadcasts

Adams, Shirley. *The Sewing Connection*.

Zieman, Nancy. *Sewing With Nancy*.

Style and Fit

Bottom, Lori, and Rhonda Chaney. *Make It Your Own*. Iola, WI: Krause Publications, 1994.

Farro, Rita. *Life Is Not a Dress Size*. Iola, WI: Krause Publications, 1996.

Larkey, Jan. *Flatter Your Figure*. New York, NY: Prentice Hall Press, 1991.

McCunn, Donald H. *How to Make Sewing Patterns*. 1st ed. Hart Publishing Co., Inc. 1973. Revised edition, 1977.

Nix-Rice, Nancy. *LOOKING GOOD, A Comprehensive Guide to Wardrobe Planning, Color and Personal Development*. Portland, OR: Palmer/Pletsch Inc., 1996.

Palmer, Pati, and Marta Alto. *Fit for Real People*. Portland, OR: Palmer/Pletsch Inc., 1998.

Zieman, Nancy. *Fitting Finesse*. Birmingham, AL: Oxmoor House, 1994.

Wearable Art

Caplinger, Mary Anne. *Weave It! Quilt It! Wear It!*. Bothell, WA: That Patchwork Place, 1996.

Dressed by the Best, Wearable Art Projects by 10 Well-Known Designers. Bothell, WA: That Patchwork Place, 1997.

Ericson, Lois, and Diane Ericson. *Design & Sew it Yourself, A Workbook for Creative Clothing*. Salem, OR: Eric's Press, 1983.

McGehee, Linda. *Texture With Textiles*. Shreveport, LA: Ghee's, 1991.

McGehee, Linda. *Creating Texture With Textiles*. Iola, WI: Krause Publications, 1998.

Murrah, Judy. *Jacket Jazz*. Bothell, WA: That Patchwork Place, 1993.

Murrah, Judy. *Jacket Jazz Encore*. Bothell, WA: That Patchwork Place, 1994.

Murrah, Judy. *More Jazz from Judy Murrah*. Bothell, WA: That Patchwork Place, 1996.

Seminole Patchwork

Bradkin, Cheryl Greider. *Basic Seminole Patchwork*. Mountain View, CA: Leone Publications, 1990.

Hanisko, Dorothy. *Simply Siminole*. Lincolnwood (Chicago), IL: The Quilt Digest Press, 1997.

Rush, Beverly and Lassie Wittman. *The Complete Book of Seminole Patchwork*. Toronto, Ontario: General Publishing Co., Ltd, 1982.

Stabilizers

Drexler, Joyce. *Sulky Secrets to Successful Stabilizing!* Harbor Heights, FL: Sulky of America, 1998.

Personal Improvement

Mallinger, Allan E. and Jeannette De Wyze. *Too Perfect - When Being in Control Gets Out of Control*. Ballantine Books, 1992.